# GERDA BENGTSSON'S BOOK OF
# DANISH STITCHERY

# GERDA BENGTSSON'S BOOK OF
# DANISH STITCHERY

## GERDA BENGTSSON
*The Danish Handcraft Guild*

VAN NOSTRAND REINHOLD COMPANY
NEW YORK   CINCINNATI   TORONTO   LONDON   MELBOURNE

Van Nostrand Reinhold Company Regional Offices:
New York   Cincinnati   Chicago   Millbrae   Dallas
Van Nostrand Reinhold Company Foreign Offices:
  London   Toronto   Melbourne

Copyright © 1972 by Litton Educational Publishing, Inc.
Library of Congress Catalog Card Number: 73-155897

All rights reserved. No part of this work covered by the copyright hereon
may be reproduced or used in any form or by any means—graphic,
electronic, or mechanical, including photocopying, recording, taping, or
information storage and retrieval systems—without written permission
of the publisher. Manufactured in the United States of America.

Designed by Visuality
Translated by Paula Hostrup-Jessen.

Published by Van Nostrand Reinhold Company
450 West 33rd Street, New York, N.Y. 10001
Published simultaneously in Canada by
Van Nostrand Reinhold Company Ltd.

16   15   14   13   12   11
10   9   8   7   6   5   4   3   2   1

# CONTENTS

Preface by Gertie Wandel   6

Introduction   7

Chapter 1. FLOWERS AND FRUITS IN CROSS-STITCH   10

Chapter 2. OTHER DESIGNS IN CROSS-STITCH   52

Chapter 3. HOW TO DESIGN FOR CROSS-STITCH   66

Chapter 4. PAPER CUTOUTS FOR CROSS-STITCH DESIGNING   92

Chapter 5. DESIGNS EMPLOYING OTHER EMBROIDERY STITCHES   100

Chapter 6. STITCHERY TECHNIQUES AND MATERIALS   120

Index   135

Diagrams for Sewing are on pp. 38, 49, 65, 74, 80, 86, 88, 90, 95, and 98

# PREFACE

As President of the Danish Handcraft Guild, to which Gerda Bengtsson has devoted her life's work, I am happy indeed to briefly introduce the Guild and one of its most important designers, Gerda Bengtsson.

Our Guild was founded in 1928, its goal being the revival of Danish needlework, hand weaving, and handicrafts. Besides display centers and shops in eight large Danish towns, the Guild runs both drawing studios and embroidery workshops, and also a school for training needlework teachers and embroidery designers. Gerda Bengtsson herself not only has her own drawing studio but also has been active as a teacher. Her embroideries are on display in the museums of many different countries and are on sale all over the world, both as finished articles and as kits. Furthermore, the entire floral world she has created has been a source of inspiration for countless embroidery designers.

The request to issue a book by Gerda Bengtsson for America was addressed to the Guild by Van Nostrand Reinhold Company, and its consultant, Mrs. R. F. Enthoven, a well-known author on American stitchery. The Guild was delighted to receive this proof of the existence of American interest in Danish stitchery, and it approached Gerda Bengtsson. She was immensely interested in the project, and the finished book reflects the eagerness and spontaneity of her working methods in creating motifs for stitching. The book is a gift to all English-speaking embroidery lovers—a gift, which for all those who appreciate it, provides a key to that stylization of nature that has characterized fine textiles from the late Middle Ages until today. It is this talent for stylizing that has placed Gerda Bengtsson's floral embroideries in a class all by themselves.

GERTIE WANDEL

# INTRODUCTION

Since I have been asked to give some account of my activities during the past thirty years and to explain how I achieved my results, a few notes on my background would seem to be appropriate.

Ever since 1940, I have been employed as a designer in the embroidery workshop of the Danish Handcraft Guild, where I was often asked how I learned to transform my flower motifs into cross-stitch patterns. The truth of the matter is that the technique developed almost spontaneously; at least, I never attended classes to learn it. Still, it didn't come about entirely by itself, for as a young girl I studied drawing and painting at the Danish Academy of Arts. At that time I had an idea I might become a landscape painter. Then one day, purely by accident, I found myself in the tapestry weaver's studio in the Academy, and I met the teacher, Mrs. Astrid Holm, a very talented painter, and saw for the first time a gigantic loom. Weaving materials were free, but there was not a single pupil! This I found rather embarrassing, so I volunteered as an apprentice weaver just for a few hours a day. Now that I had the opportunity to make full use of my sense of color and form, my interest in the subject grew rapidly. The motifs to be woven were transferred to the web on the loom, and the way in which a pattern was developed proved to be very similar to the technique for making cross-stitch patterns.

Thereafter I spent eight months in Paris. The study of the old French tapestries of "The Lady and the Unicorn" ("La dame à licorne") was a great experience. I managed to copy several details from these medieval masterpieces—chiefly the animal and flower motifs—in watercolor, and learned a great deal thereby. Each plant is a work of art in itself, irregular yet balanced, with beautiful line and fascinating color. One motif, of a rabbit jumping among flowers, I made into a cross-stitch pattern at the request of the Handcraft Guild, which, in 1928, had just opened a small showroom at 20 Nyhavn in Copenhagen. This was the very small beginning, but of course I didn't really intend to specialize in medieval flowers. I retained their simplicity of line, however, and this influence is revealed in much of my later work.

Some years later I hit on the idea of using the Danish flora for my cross-stitch patterns. I first thought of doing the embroidery on canvas, but some people at the Guild embroidery workshop thought the pattern would show up to greater advantage on coarse linen embroidered with cotton thread and with the background left unworked. The result was a success, for the flowers had a lightness and charm that reflected the most becoming aspect of these delicate wild plants. I felt encouraged to continue along these lines. Soon I was given a job in the embroidery workshop and took up the study of wild flowers in earnest, making drawings and paintings of them and, in time, establishing my own herbarium and botanical library. In nature I found innumerable motifs.

Another great source of inspiration over the years was the collection of beautifully dyed yarns, which formed an impressive array of samples on the workshop shelves. They were the work of the Guild's dyer, Mr. Ejnar Hansen, and although synthetically dyed, closely approached his chart of vegetable dyes. I shall never forget his herbarium, its vegetable dyes, and numerous bits of yarn in manifold hues fastened to the appropriate plants.

All this is part of my artistic background.

In addition, I have taught embroidery design in the School of the Danish Handcraft Guild for twenty-four years. Although the work was most interesting, it presented great problems. The students—young girls training to become needlework teachers—naturally differed greatly with regard to their talent for drawing and painting. Besides copying and embroidering classical needlework, they were required to create new designs for execution in the school, and the latter task proved the most difficult one. There were some students who were talented and could easily be taught, but others needed constant prodding to get them going at all. At last, I succeeded in getting them to create something on their own the day I thought of letting them cut out motifs in white paper. [See Chapter 4.] Christmastime was approaching and the students thought that they were supposed to make Christmas decorations out of the white paper—a notion of theirs that I didn't dispel, since they were enjoying themselves like children. In this way I discovered that many students, though unable to draw, were very clever with scissors, inspiring each other to greater and greater efforts.

The best of the paper cutouts were used as a basis for new embroideries. We discussed which needlework technique would be the most suitable in each case, and I really believe the students felt they had helped to create something new. When I left my job at the School, it was solely to be able to devote more time to the designing of my own patterns. Moreover, the various books on cross-stitch issued by the Danish Handcraft Guild demanded more and more of my time.

In this book, I describe my working methods not in order to encourage people to adopt my own particular style, but to help those who have the inclination and ability to undertake something similar. I also believe that many who imagine themselves quite unable to draw and have never tried may find it a help to study both Chapter 4, which deals with cutting out motifs, and Chapter 3, on how to create cross-stitch designs. If I have not included any pictures taken from the botanical works I have sometimes used as sources for my work, it is because the procedure is exactly the same as when I use my own watercolors as models.

Whenever designs have been drawn especially for this book, diagrams for sewing have been provided, as well as full information with regard to materials and measurements. It should be noted, however, that all measurements are only approximate. For some of the embroideries I have added information that might possibly be of interest; in other cases I have merely indicated the finished measurements and materials required. It is my hope that the contents of this book will be a source of inspiration to all needlework lovers and to those who feel an urge to create something on their own.

Finally, I wish to express my most cordial thanks to a fine teacher of needlework, Baroness Marianne Lotzbeck, who collaborated with me in working out the text for the various embroidery techniques in this book.

"The Lady and the Unicorn," a sixteenth-century tapestry to be found at the Cluny Museum in France.

*Chapter 1.*

# FLOWERS AND FRUITS IN CROSS-STITCH

## MODELS

For some years all my designs were motifs taken from florae that I used as models. In some ways this was easy, although nothing could be used exactly as I found it; it always had to be adapted for the specific purpose. In the long run, however, this method was not altogether satisfying, so I decided to paint my own models. Since this meant having to go out to find the plants, I joined the Danish Botanical Society and enjoyed many a long tramp in field and forest, taking plants home with me, which I subsequently drew or pressed. After a while I managed to collect a herbarium of plants which was quite suitable for my purpose. Unfortunately, herbarium specimens are not always satisfactory as models, for both color and form are frequently lost. Nevertheless the specimen can provide a good starting point; it is always possible to consult a flora, preferably several at a time, in order to obtain the best results.

The most important thing is to have a thorough knowledge of the plants you want to draw, and so the best idea is to pick a plant or dig it up and put it right on the table in front of you while you are drawing. I must admit, however, that you have to hurry with the drawing before the plant withers. Even at this early stage you can simplify what you see and adapt it for your own purposes.

## COMPOSITIONS

I divide my own compositions based on plant motifs into two groups:
1. The free composition.
2. The repeat.

With the free composition I endeavor to distribute the design harmoniously within the area which has to be filled. There must be a balanced distribution of spatial units and color and there must be a good rhythmic line. By balance I do not mean symmetry, since I consider perfect symmetry to be ugly and at variance with nature.

As to the composition called the repeat, it is drawn in such a way that the pattern can be repeated indefinitely. It can be drawn on the slant, straight, or in an irregular sequence. Within a certain number of threads, you can work freely, but at the transition point from one repeat to another, you are restricted to letting each repeat begin precisely as the previous one, and this must be done so naturally that the restriction cannot be sensed.

1-1. Free composition.
Cushion, spring flowers, from *Cross-Stitch Embroidery II,* published by the Danish Handcraft Guild in 1956.
Size: 11″ x 11⅜″.
Danish Flower Thread on linen IA.

1-2. Repeat; bellpull with black currant.

In the embroidery in Fig. 1-1, only the background is worked, and the most important contours are outlined by a few backstitches. I call this kind of pattern a negative, because it is the reverse of all the other embroideries stitched on linen, in which the motif is embroidered and the background remains unworked. The cushion is sewn in red, shade No. 88. (See pp. 122-123 for the illustration of Danish Flower Threads.)

The bellpull in Fig. 1-2 consists of 8 repeats, one of which is illustrated. The design was drawn from life, and the colors kept as close to the original as possible. The complete bellpull is shown in Fig. 1-3.

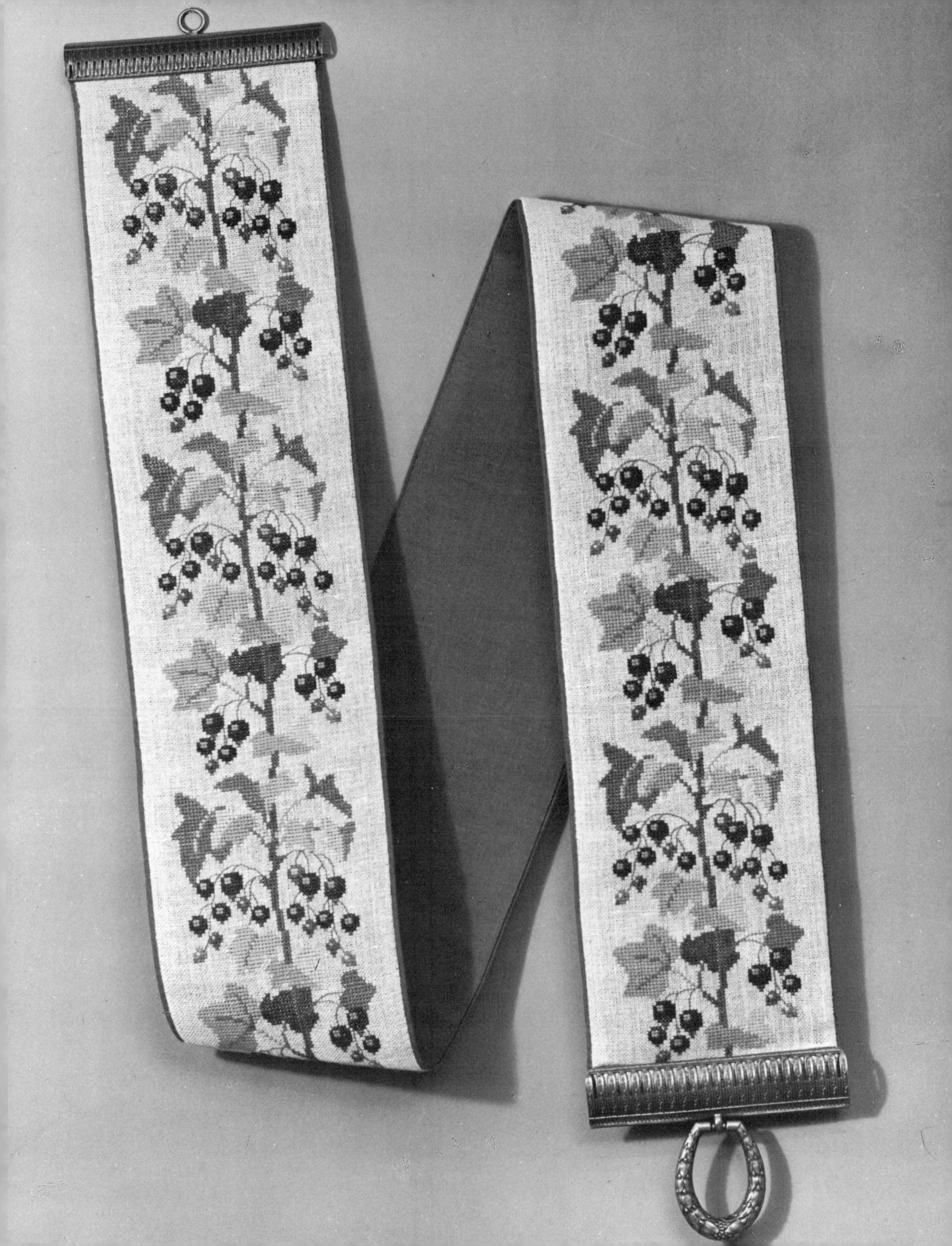

*Facing page,* 1-3. Bellpull with black currants, L.N. 3271.
Size: 4¼" x 50¾".
Danish Flower Thread on linen II, unbleached.

1-4. Wall hanging, 12 flowers, L.N. 3624.
Size: approximately 21" x 16⅛".
Danish Flower Thread on linen IA.

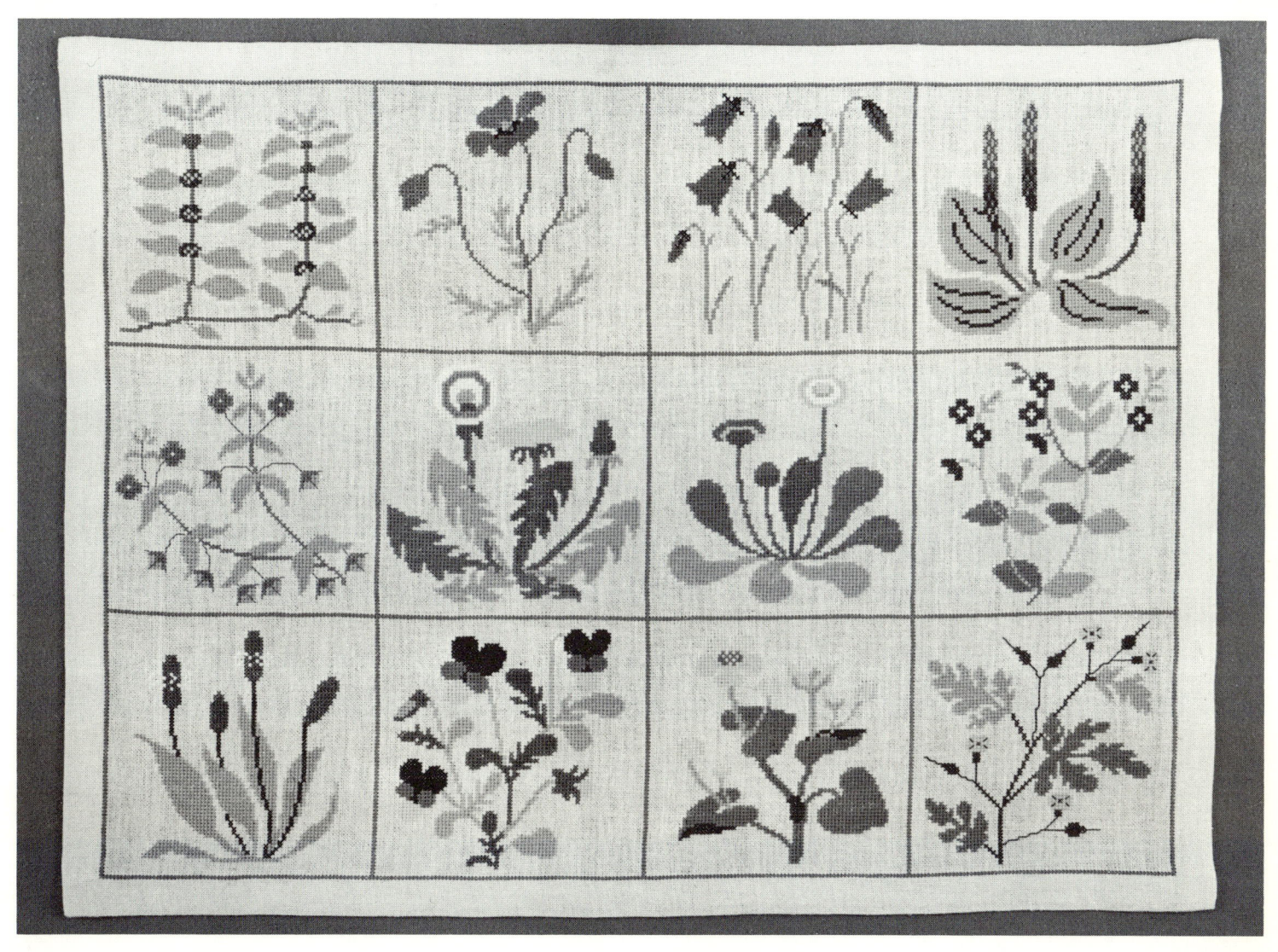

On the top row of Fig. 1-4 the flowers are corn mint, poppy, harebell, plantain. The middle row has the scarlet pimpernel, dandelion, daisy, speedwell. The ribwort plantain, pansy, marsh marigold, herb robert are on the bottom row. I drew these 12 flower motifs in 1935, with the help of botanical textbooks, though I adapted the models so that each one fitted into its own square. Each motif was used in a doily. Later on I drew an additional 24 flowers, retaining the original colors as much as possible.

The wall hanging was made in 1969 in order to display the original simple motifs in a new way, and on a coarser material.

13

Intended for working on canvas, the 3 embroidery designs for cushions and tapestry (see Figs 1-5 through 1-7) are based on my copies of the "Lady with the Unicorn" in the Cluny Museum.

The tapestry is drawn in repeats, i.e., the pattern can be continued by adding a repeat in either direction. On examining the tapestry more closely it is possible to make out 2 different sections, however.

The tapestry is worked on coarse canvas with double thread and made up of 6 sections sewn together. The cushions are worked on a finer canvas, but with single thread of the same quality and color.

1-5. Cushion with flowers on a blue background, L.N. 3284A.
Size: 14" x 14".
Woolen yarn on canvas No. 24.

1-6. Cushion with flowers on a blue background, L.N. 3284B.
Size: 14" x 14".
Woolen yarn on canvas No. 24.

*Facing page,* 1-7. Tapestry with flowers on a blue background, L.N. 3284.
Size: 41" x 61½"; 6 sections, 20½" x 20½" each.
Woolen yarn on canvas No. 16.

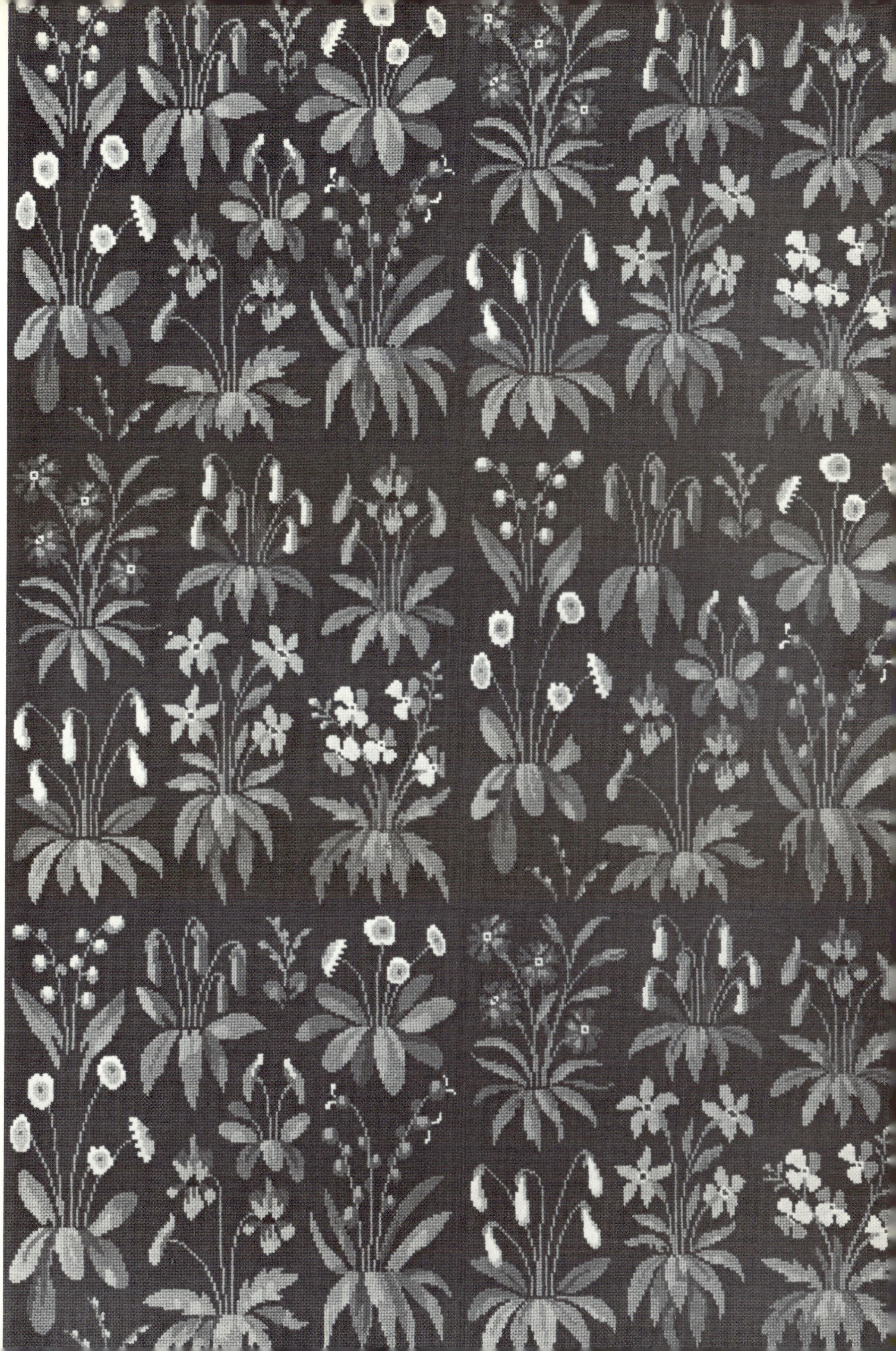

1-8. Tea cozy, wild flowers, L.N. 1662.
Size: 9¾" x 13½".
Danish Flower Thread on linen I.

The embroidery shown in Fig. 1-9 has been bought by the Danish Museum of Decorative Art.

*Facing page, top,* 1-9. Wall hanging, lady's-mantle, L.N. 1873B.
Size: 16½" x 21¼".
Danish Flower Thread on linen 1A.

*Facing page, bottom,* 1-10. Wall hanging, wild flowers, L.N. 3614.
Size: 18¼" x 23".
Danish Flower Thread on linen 10.5.

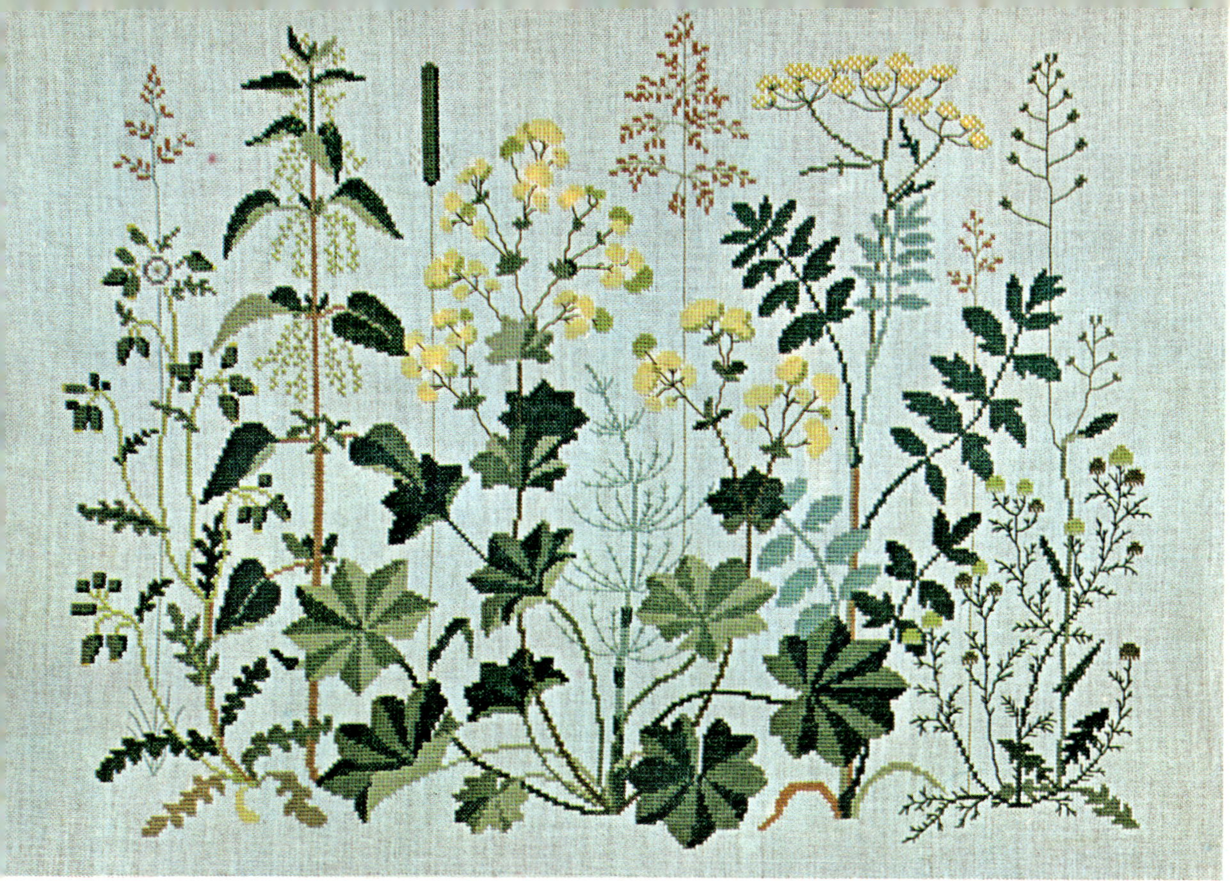

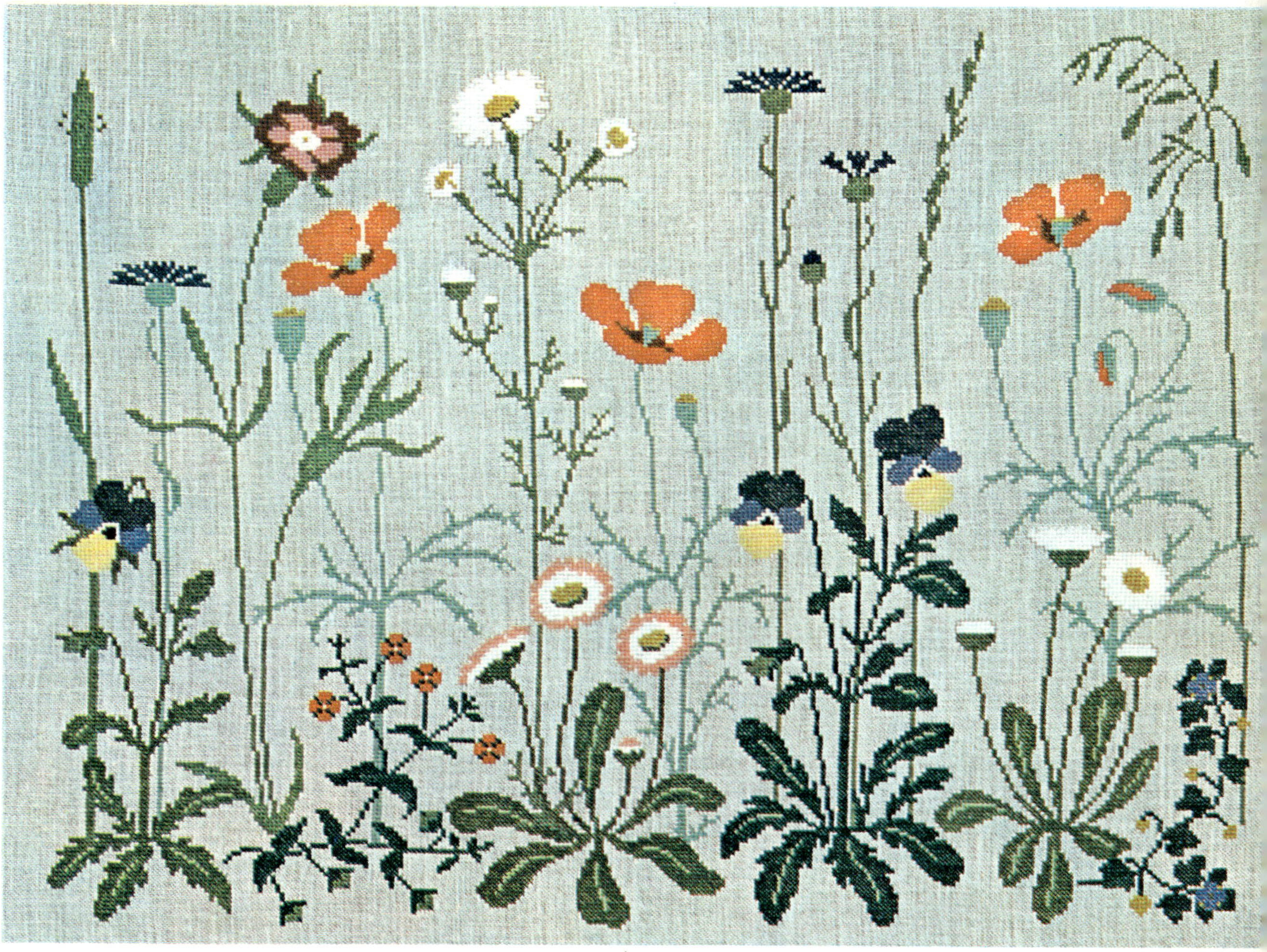

1-11. Tablecloth, wreath of ivy, central part—L.N. 2866.
Tablecloth measurements: 51" x 51".
The wreath measures 17¼" in diameter.
Danish Flower Thread on linen II.

The tablecloth shown above is drawn in 4 identical sections, i.e., 4 repeats. First I measured out on the cloth the number of stitches I had at my disposal. The 2 diameters at right angles that I then drew were very helpful in working out the repeat, which runs in a circle, and finally ends up where it began. The leaves are in pale, medium, and dark shades of green, and the stems are in brown.

The 6 flowers in Fig. 1-12 are drawn from the 36 flowers described on page 13, but they are shorter by 20 stitches and thus simpler to sew. The color scheme is the same. From top to bottom on the left, they are: lady's mantle, forget-me-not, lungwort; on the right: marsh marigold, pansy, scarlet pimpernel.

1-12. Place mats with flowers, corner motifs, L.N. 1677.
Size: 11¾" x 16½".
Danish Flower Thread on linen II, bleached.

1-13. Wall hanging, black mullein,
L.N. 3602.
Size: 25" x 43".
Danish Flower Thread on linen 10.5.

The large plant (approximately 38" long) seen on this page was sent to me in a box, carefully wrapped in wet paper. It was cut into several pieces, and quantities of beautiful yellow flowers dropped off during the unpacking, so I was obliged to hurry up and draw them. As much as possible I used the plant's natural colors for this pattern.

In the spring, 1970, the embroidery was bought by The Danish Museum of Decorative Art.

I based my pattern of the runner mainly on pressed plants with violet, blue, and red flowers. However, in my design, I confined myself to shades of green and yellow.

1-14. Runner, green plants, L.N. 2008.
Size: 22¼" x 39¼".
Danish Flower Thread on linen 1.

1-15. Pressed plant, primrose; herbarium: Lois Fog.

*Facing page,* 1-17. 12 wall hangings, wild plants, L.N. 2762.
Size: 13″ x 21¼″.
Danish Flower Thread on linen 10.5.

The pressed plant of the primrose formed the model for the cushion design in Fig. 1-16. (See p. 24.) In working out the pattern I paid great attention to line and balance. I bent the stiff leaf in the middle a little bit to the left and added an entirely new one. Finally came the distribution of color. Almost all the bright yellow flowers are on the right side of the pressed plant. However, I rearranged this in my drawing so that the colors would be more evenly distributed.

It was winter when the design was drawn and since the flowers on the pressed plant had lost their original shape, I had to consult a botany textbook.

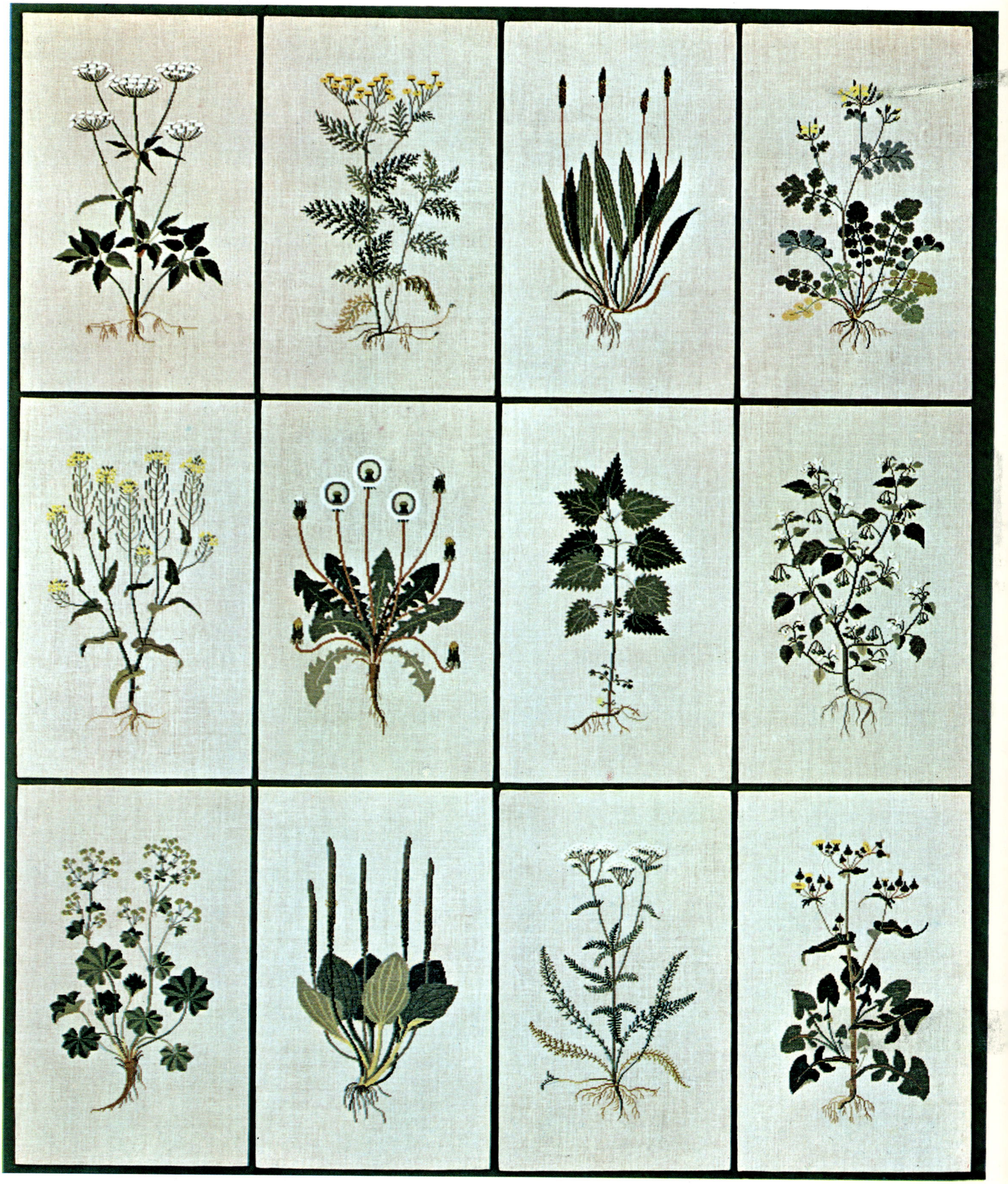

1-16. Cushion, primrose, L.N. 3557.
Size: 12½" x 15¼".
Danish Flower Thread on linen D, unbleached.

One summer I started on the series shown in Fig. 1-17. (See p. 23.) At first I only meant to draw 6 plants, and that was very quickly accomplished. I took the motifs from my country garden, where plantains, dandelions, stinging nettles, goutweed, milfoil, and tansy lead a fairly peaceful existence.

When I had finished these 6 plants, I found there was enough time to draw 6 more. But now a problem arose: I had chosen only white, yellow, and green plants and wished to continue in this way. Where would I find another 6 plants in the same colors and size as the first ones? I had to look elsewhere, for there is a natural limit as to what my garden can supply me with in the way of weeds.

1-18. Life-size detail of one of the flowers in Fig. 1-19.

It took time; autumn came and I lacked only one plant. It was a yellow one, and I decided upon yellow celandine. But I searched in vain; it looked as if I would have to make do with my previous cross-stitch embroideries and find the pictures I could in the botanical books. There wasn't a single picture showing the roots, however; so now I was in a proper dilemma.

I suddenly remembered that celandine grows around people's country houses. So I made a journey to the nearest village, and—to be sure—I saw several withered plants there. Only the rosette at the bottom remained, but the important thing was that I had the root now and could conclude the series.

The top row of Fig. 1-17 shows, from left to right: goutweed, tansy, narrow-leaved plantain, greater celandine. The middle row has: rutabaga, dandelion, nettle, black nightshade. At the bottom are: lady's-mantle, broad-leaved plantain, milfoil, sow thistle.

25

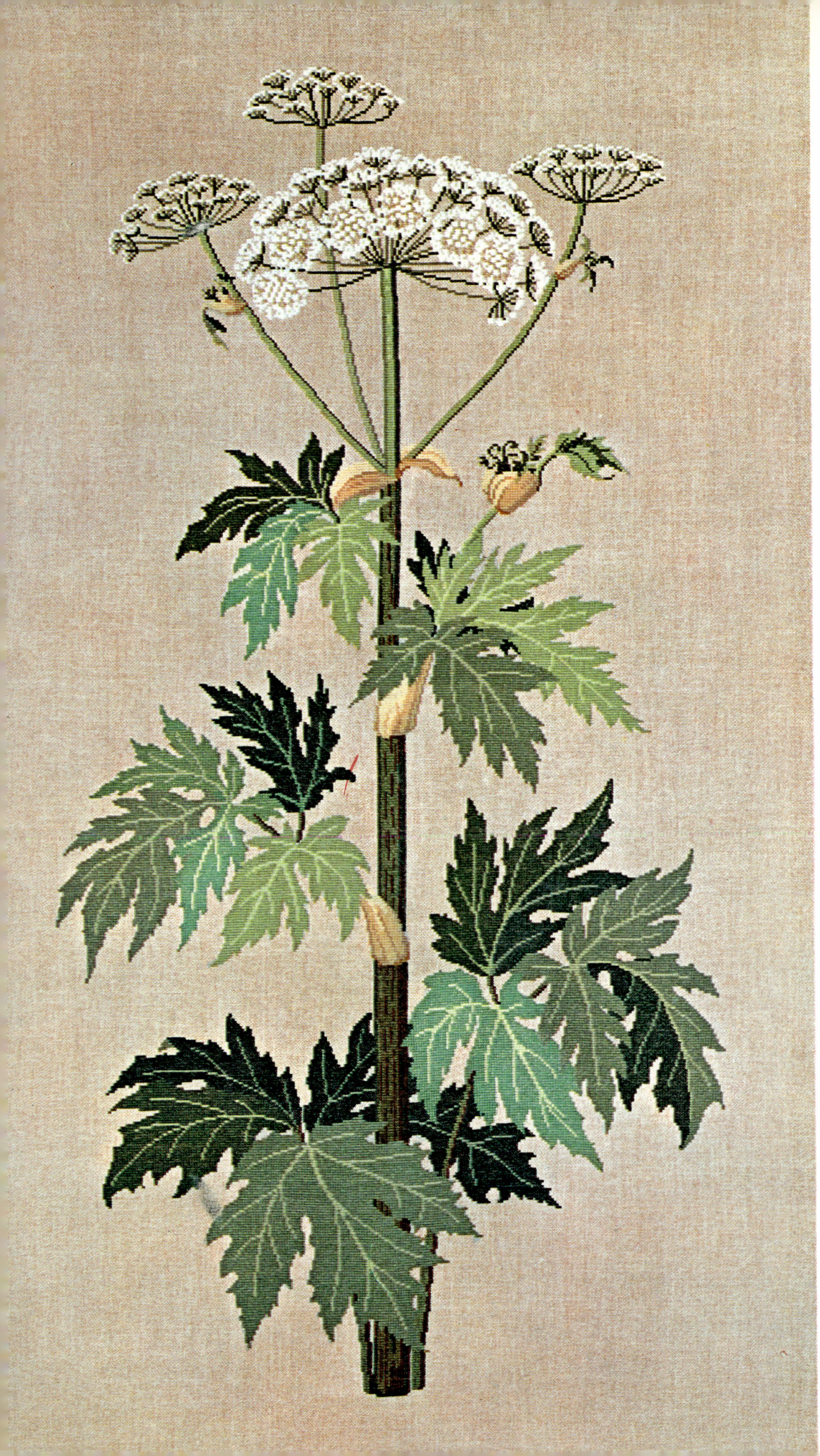

One day I was given the top of a large cow parsnip by some guests whom I had invited to my summerhouse on the condition that they bring me a cow parsnip. I was just about to start drawing a couple of specimens from my garden when I discovered that the tops were not quite good enough. The cut-off specimen was put in a bucket of water, and then it was a matter of getting the drawing finished before the plant withered. The pattern seen here was worked out from 3 different plants.

    I had already decided that the design should be worked on linen D, unbleached, and with 2 threads, so that I would have the advantage of being able to put 2 different colors together and use them for the plant's thick stem, which is both mottled and spotted in its original state.

    This embroidery (Fig. 1-19) involves a great deal of work, but it is not very difficult; even men have ventured to tackle it.

Fig. 1-20 shows yet another repeating pattern in which the elements are irregularly spaced as in the tapestry on a blue background on page 15. In drawing this pattern I used both florae, pressed plants, and some of my earlier motifs, adapting them so that they would fit into the design. The wall hanging is mainly worked in green, with isolated touches of yellow, white, and reddish tones.

*Facing page,* 1-19. Tapestry: cow parsnip, L.N. 3260.
Size: 37″ x 65″.
Danish Flower Thread on linen D, unbleached.

1-20. Wall hanging, wild flowers, L.N. 3564.
Size: 24¾″ x 25″.
Danish Floral Thread on linen 10.5.

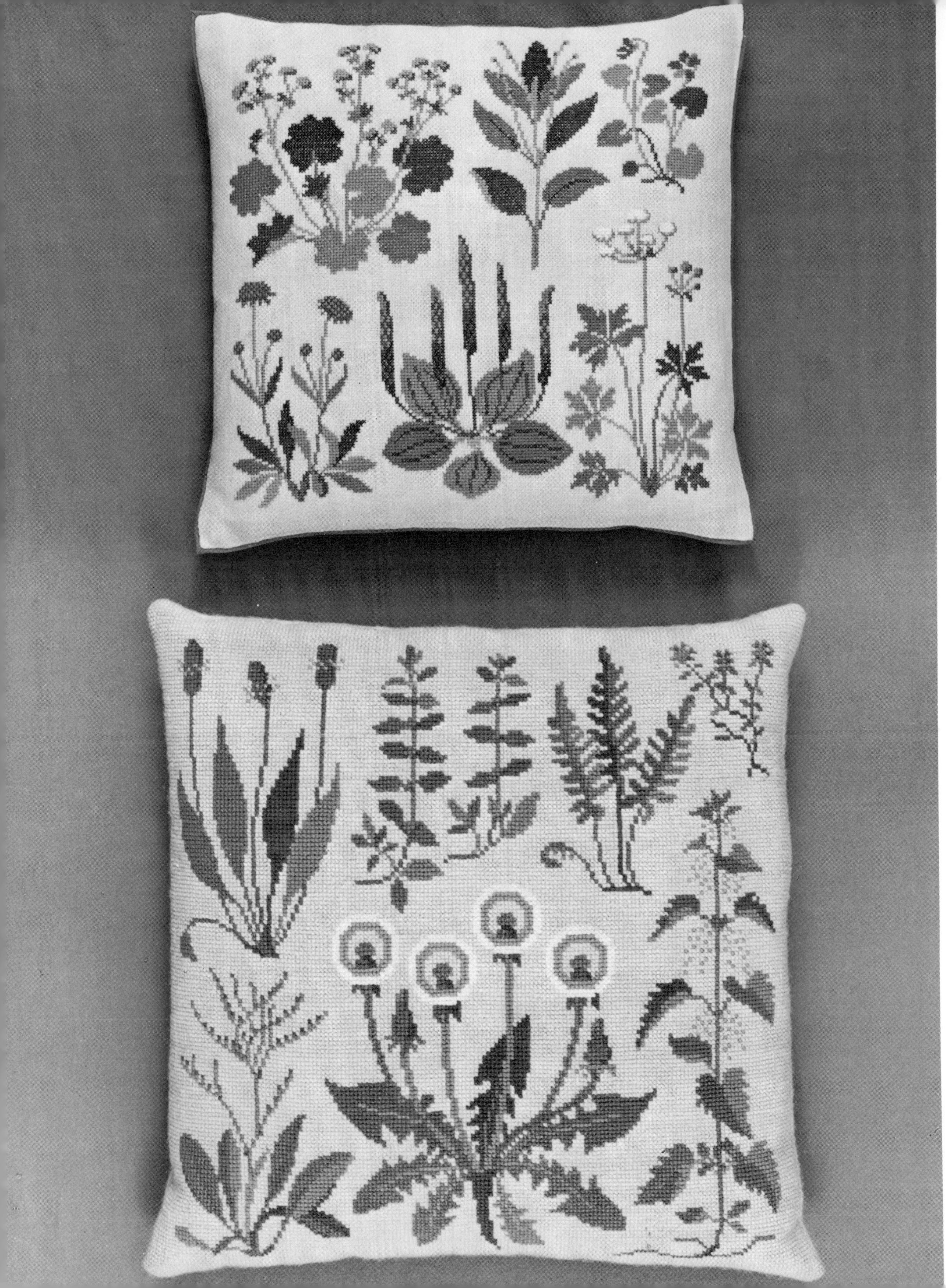

# HOW MY GOOSEBERRY CUSHION CAME TO BE MADE

Our yarn file in the Handcraft Guild contains a very beautiful collection of Ejnar Hansen's dyed cotton yarns—Danish Flower Thread. (See pp. 122-123.) The green range has once or twice inspired me to create designs worked entirely in green. One day I suddenly had the urge to design a cross-stitch pattern with gooseberries, but where was I to lay hands on them? It was winter, and as I cannot draw without using a model, my creative dreams were frustrated. Spring finally came, and my longing to get started drove me to the countryside, into my sister's garden in Rungsted. Alas, the gooseberry bushes were only just in bloom. Three weeks later I was back with my watercolors and paper. Although it was still too early, I cut off a branch of unripe berries, stuck it in a vase, painted it in a purely naturalistic manner, and a few days later made the first sketch for the gooseberry pattern. I had always envisaged the design as being on the slant, so I used the oblique branch as my point of reference, though it had to be greatly simplified and changed. The transition from one branch to the next, as well as the beginning and end of the design had to be correctly connected and composed. The unripe berries, which in my watercolor sketch were as much bloom as fruit, I redesigned as ripe berries.

Before the cushion was stitched, I made a small sample in which I worked the repeating pattern together with a small portion of the repeats on both the left and on the right. Thus I could be certain of the effect of all the colors I had determined to use.

The first model of the gooseberry cushion was bought by the Danish Museum of Decorative Art in 1947.

*Facing page, top,* 1-21. Cushion with wild flowers, L.N. 3562A.
Size: 13" x 13 3/8".
Danish Flower Thread on linen 10.5.
You will recognize one section of the wall hanging shown in Fig. 1-20 in this cushion, which is made of the same materials.

*Facing page, bottom,* 1-22. Pillow with wild flowers, L.N. 3572B.
Size: 15¼" x 15½".
Woolen yarn on canvas No. 24.
Here is the other section of the wall hanging in Fig. 1-20, this time sewn on a cushion made of canvas.

1-23. Gooseberry branch in watercolor and pencil.

1-24. This section of the gooseberry cushion, life-size, is 5¾" x 8½". As shown, it is slightly less than life-size.

1-25. Cushion, gooseberry, L.N. 1979.
Size: 15¾" x 16½".
Danish Flower Thread on linen II, unbleached.

*Facing page,* 1-26. Red currant branch in watercolor.

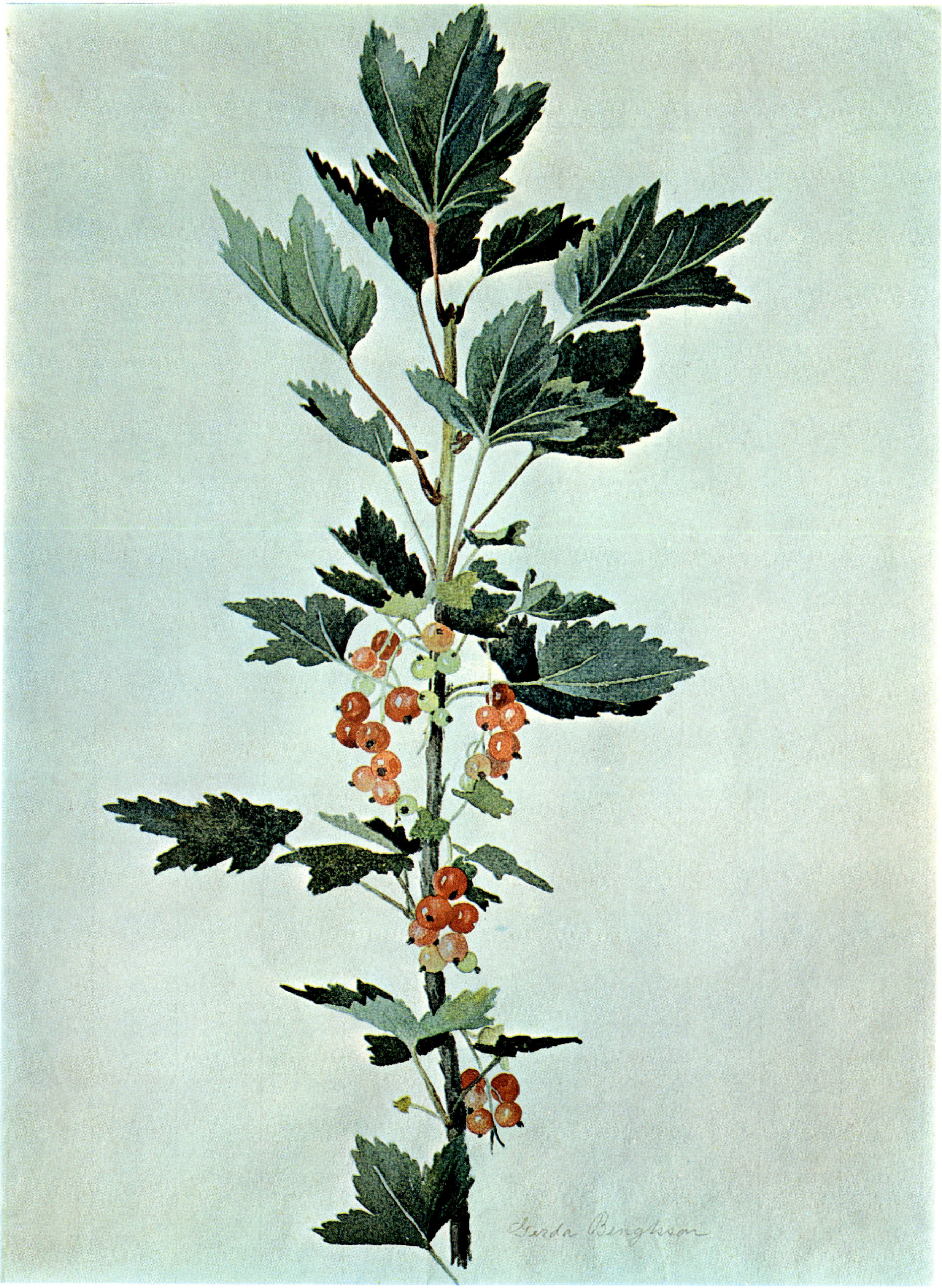
Gerda Bengtsson

1-27. Cushion with red currants, L.N. 2111.
Size: 19" x 17".
Danish Flower Thread on linen II, unbleached.

The gooseberry pattern gave me the idea of drawing one with red currants. Again, it was to be a cushion, but this time I wanted to lay out the pattern in several blocks, as in the traditional block print patterns.

Once more I found myself in the same garden in Rungsted, but just as before I had arrived too early; the berries were still unripe. However, this time I discovered at once that this was in fact a great advantage. Unripe red currants are more picturesque than ripe ones.

I cut a branch off and placed it upright in a vase, as it was my idea that the pattern should repeat itself in vertical oblong blocks. You can see the branch painted in watercolor in Fig. 1-26.

I thereupon began the preliminary sketches. It is not always possible to stick slavishly to one's starting point. I rejected the first sketches immediately, the vertical branch appearing stiff and uninteresting when repeated. So I bent the branch on the drawing, but berries and leaves naturally had to follow after. It isn't sufficient to draw one block, and then believe that it can be repeated without further ado. The block must be so composed that the repeats on all sides are good. I thought that was the most difficult thing about this pattern.

This embroidery earned me the gold medal at the Triennale in Milan in 1951.

1-29. Cushion with sunflowers, L.N. 2749.
Finished measurements: 12½" x 14½".
Danish Flower Thread on linen IA.
In this repeating pattern, I've confined the colors to shades of bright yellow, gold, and green.

1-28. Wall hanging with sunflowers, L.N. 2767.
Finished measurements: 9" x 38½".
Danish Flower Thread on linen D, bleached.
The effect of the motif here on coarse canvas is bolder than as it appears on the cushion in Fig. 1-29.

1-30. Canvas cushion, lady's-mantle,
L.N. 3553.
Finished measurements: 14¼" x 14¾".
Woolen yarn on canvas No. 24.

1-31. Chair seat with lady's-mantle,
L.N. 3553.
The same motif and materials have been
used as in the preceding cushion.
Length of chair seat: 16½" x 16½".
Width: 12¾" at back.
      15¾" in front.

1-32. One third of the pattern which is illustrated in full in Fig. 1-34.

35

1-33. Life-size detail of Fig. 1-32.

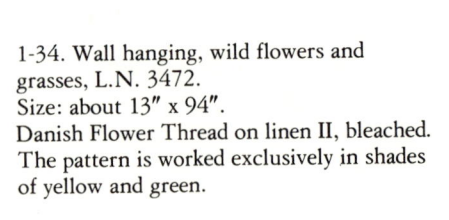

1-34. Wall hanging, wild flowers and grasses, L.N. 3472.
Size: about 13" x 94".
Danish Flower Thread on linen II, bleached. The pattern is worked exclusively in shades of yellow and green.

36

The embroidery (Fig. 1-34) was shown in Australia in an exhibit entitled "1968 Design in Scandinavia." That same year it was also shown as part of the Danish Arts and Crafts Exhibition at the Victoria and Albert Museum in London.

I feel that the Danish Flower Threads that are available to me contribute greatly to the effect of my designs, and you may order these same threads from the Danish Handcraft Guild (see p. 134). However, if you want to match your own threads with the Danish Flower Thread colors, you may do so by consulting the illustration of the Danish Flower Threads on pp. 122-123, in which the threads are identified by number.

1-35. Cushion, wild rose, L.N. 2944E, from state flowers of the United States. Size: 11¾" x 11¾".
Danish Flower Thread on linen IA.

# SUNFLOWER
## KANSAS

No. 15

| 216 | 6 | 31 | 48 | 203 | 206 | 212 | 34 | 40 | 10 | 100 | 228 | 215 |

38

*Facing page,* 1-36. Wall hanging, sunflower,
L.N. 2970. Color drawing on graph paper.
Size: 8½" x 7".
Cutting measurement: 12" x 10½".
Material of wall hanging: Linen IA.
Danish Flower Thread, single thread.

For the pattern in Fig. 1-36, measure a point on the material 2" in and 2" down at the top left-hand corner. Begin working the border here according to the drawing, with blue No. 228. No. 15 is the serial number of the motif. The finished wall hanging can be fixed on cardboard, leaving an edge 8 threads wide outside the border all the way around. (See instructions for the cross-stitch on p. 124, and for designing with the cross-stitch, p. 66.)

## STATE FLOWERS OF THE UNITED STATES

In 1961 I was given a very difficult job. I was asked to design the 50 state flowers of the United States for a design in cross-stitch.

With the help of the head gardener of the Danish Botanical Garden I learned the names of the flowers and was given the lists of the florae in which there was a good chance the flowers might be found. There was, of course, no question of a lengthy journey to all the states in order to draw from life. So, with the help of librarians, botanists, and friends, I was lent many beautiful books.

Several color slides were sent to me from America, and these were very useful as models. It was with great relief that I found I knew several of the flowers; these I could pick when the time was right. I obtained the sunflower from my neighbor's garden and a Californian poppy from the butcher's garden. It took me a couple of years to assemble them all.

The two big wall hangings in Figs. 1-37 and 1-38 were exhibited at the Cooper Union Museum in New York in 1962. All the flowers were shown in the October 1964 issue of *Woman's Day.*

Some of the motifs are suitable for working on cushions of linen IA, while other motifs can be worked on the coarser linen D, unbleached. All the motifs can be sewn separately as small wall hangings on linen IA, bleached. For illustrations of the linens that I use and information on the equivalent material that can be obtained, see pages 120-121.

1-37. Wall hanging, 25 state flowers of the United States, L.N. 2970.
Size: 35½" x 43".
Linen IA.

1-38. Wall hanging, 25 state flowers of the
United States, L.N. 2970.
Size: 35½" x 43".
Linen IA.

1-39. Cushion, sagebrush, from state
flowers of the United States, **L.N.** 3659.
Size: 11¾″ x 11¾″.
Danish Flower Thread on wool canvas.

The wool canvas (Fig. 1-39) is slightly yellow and has 18 threads to the inch. Not all the state flowers look their best when worked on this material.

1-40. Wall hanging, American Beauty Rose, L.N. 2970.
Size: 7″ x 8½″.
Material: Linen IA, Danish Flower Thread, single thread.

1-41. Place mat with African marigold from *The Year's Cross-Stitch, 1966,* published by the Danish Handcraft Guild. The pattern for the place mat is given in Fig. 1-45.

44

In Fig. 1-42 on the next page, the top row has, from left to right:
January—winter jasmine.
February—snowdrop.
March—hazel.

Second row:
April—daffodil.
May—narcissus.
June—African marigold.

Third row:
July—rose.
August—Senecio clivorum.
September—Helenium.

Fourth row:
October—small-leaved lime.
November—chrysanthemum.
December—Christmas rose.

On the top row in Fig. 1-43 (p. 47), from left to right, are:
January—ivy; February—alder; March—sweet violet.
Second row:
April—anemone; May—beech; June—dog rose.
Third row:
July—woody nightshade; August—hop;
September—vine.
Fourth row:
October—Virginia creeper; November—ivy with
fruits; December—holly.

*Overleaf*, 1-42. These 12 doilies are also in *The Year's Cross-Stitch, 1966*.
Doily size: 6⅓" x 6⅓".
Danish Flower Thread on linen IA.

*On p. 47*, 1-43. Wreaths calendar for 1967 in the form of 12 doilies.
Doily size: 6" x 6".
Danish Flower Thread on linen IA.

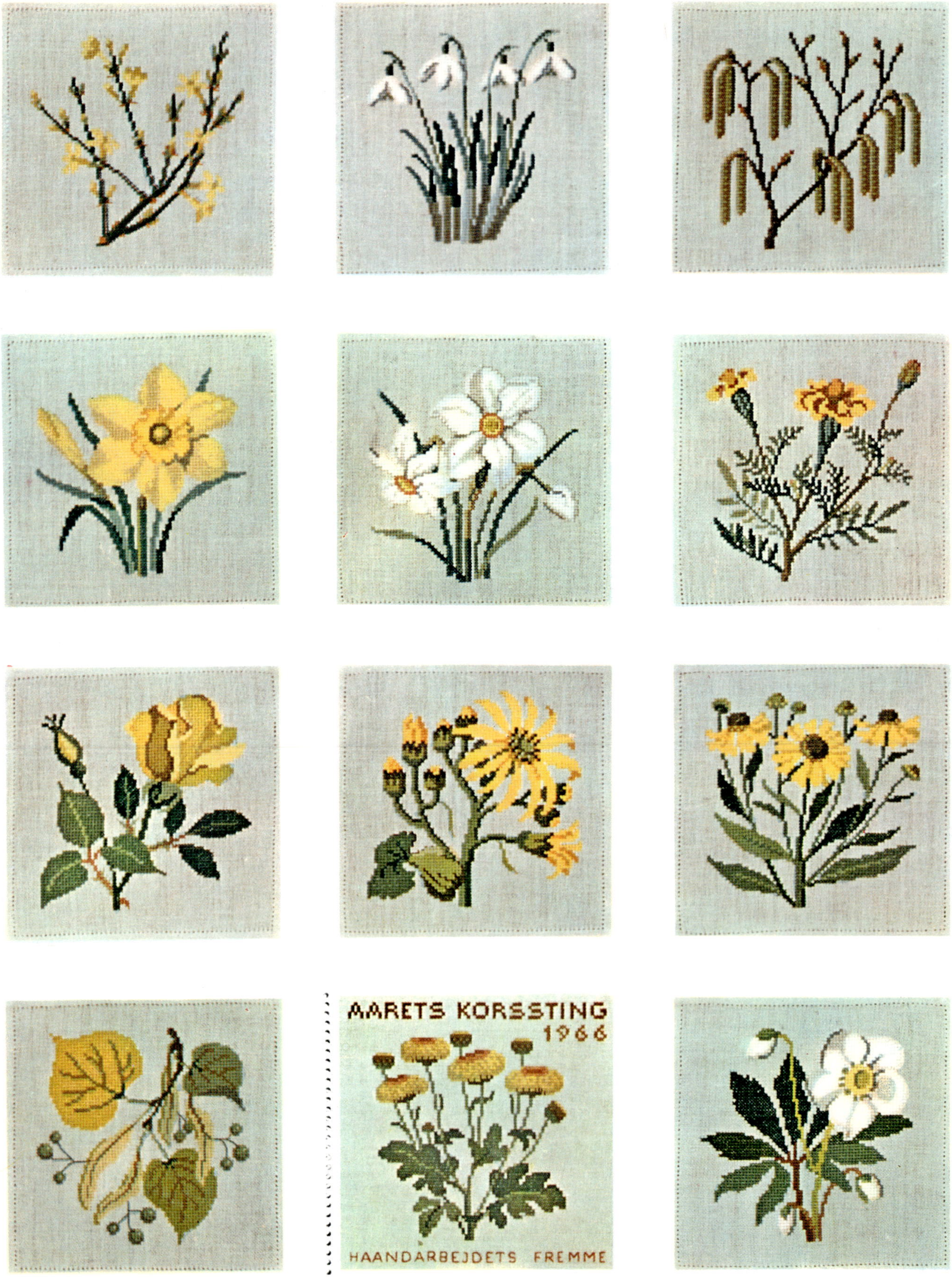
AARETS KORSSTING
1966
HAANDARBEJDETS FREMME

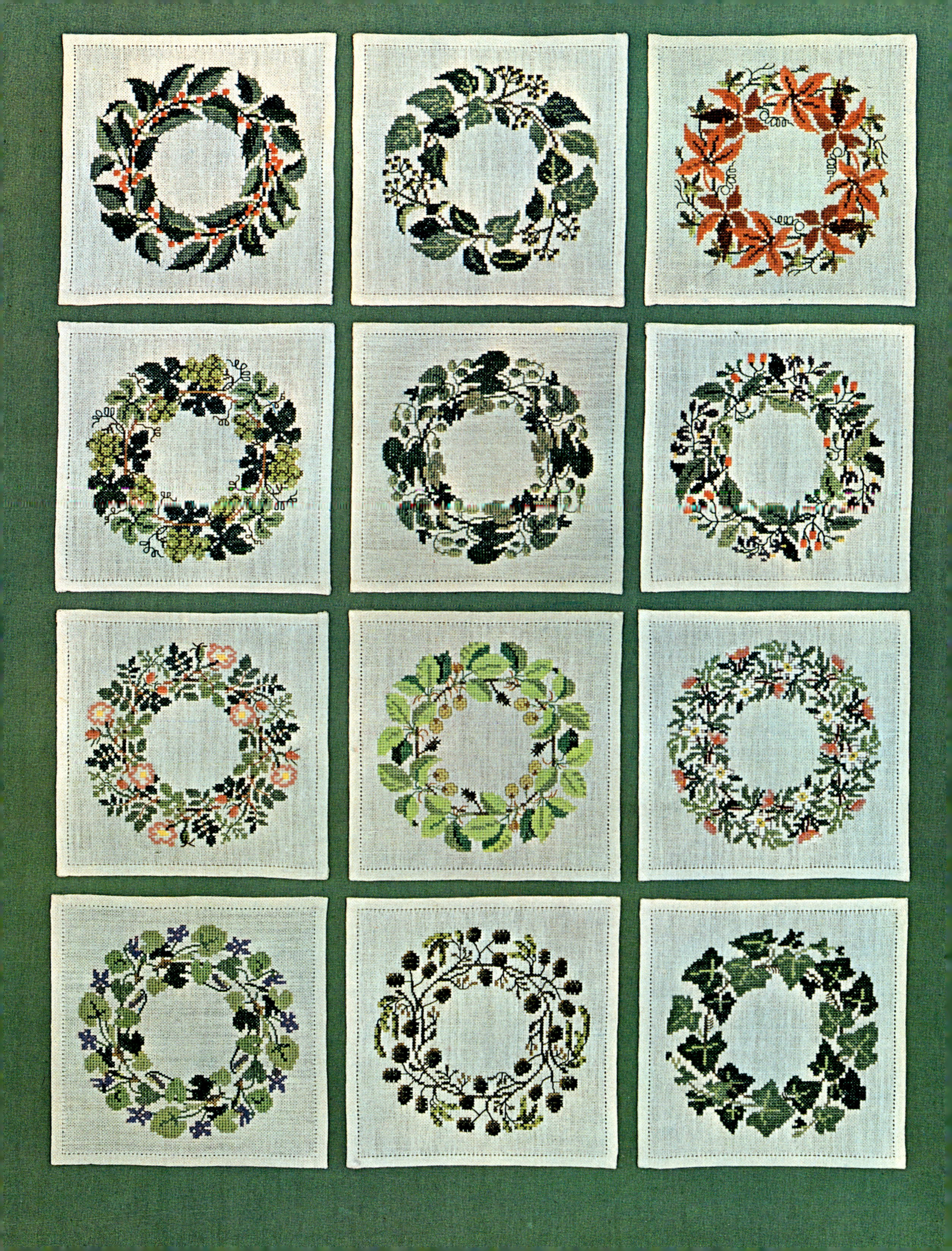

1-44. Cushion, Virginia creeper.
Size: 13" x 13".
Flower Thread on linen D, unbleached.
(See Fig. 1-46 for the sewing pattern.)

For the pattern in Fig. 1-45, begin on the border with color No. 10 in the top right-hand corner, 1" in and down. The border measures 502 threads long and 382 threads across, which equal 251 stitches x 191 stitches. The hem is 8 threads wide. Seam it in the usual manner right up to the border.

To sew the cushion in Fig. 1-46, find the midpoint of the material, which corresponds to the midpoint of the pattern. Count from the center along the midline outward to the nearest leaf or flower and begin to work the motif from there. One square on the design paper equals 2 threads on the material.

1-45. Sewing pattern for place mat with African marigold (from *The Year's Cross-Stitch,* 1966).
Cutting measurements: 12" x 17".
Material: Linen IA.
Thread: Danish Flower Thread, single thread.

1-46. Sewing pattern for cushion with Virginia creeper from 1967 calendar.
Cutting measurements: 2 pieces, 16¼" x 16¼" each.
Finished measurements: 13" x 13".
Thread: Danish Flower Thread, used double.
Materials: Canvas D, bleached.
Technique: Cross-stitch and backstitch.
(For designing with the backstitch, see pp. 66 and 67.)

49

50

*Facing page,* 1-47. Place mats with fruits, corner motifs, L.N. 3293.
Size: 11¾" x 16½".
Danish Flower Thread on linen I.

1-48. Mat for table center with ivy pattern, L.N. 2043. Approximately half is shown.
Size: 17¾" x 17¾".
Danish Flower Thread on linen I.

From left to right, the fruits shown in Fig. 1-47 are: rose hips and elderberries on top; blueberries and gooseberries in the middle; and hawthorn berries and red currants at the bottom.

The ivy pattern for Fig. 1-48 is drawn in four identical parts, that is, four repeats. The border is continuous, as in the mats shown in Fig. 1-47. For the corner motif I used the fruits and top of an ivy plant, where the leaves were differently shaped than those on the remainder of the plant. The color scheme is the same as in Fig. 1-11 (p. 18), but the linen is finer.

# Chapter 2.
# OTHER DESIGNS IN CROSS-STITCH

Although flowers in cross-stitch are my own special interest, I have also done some work with motifs inspired by old Danish samplers. My first samples were almost copies of them. What interested me most were the tiny, stiff human figures combined with flowers, trees, birds, animals, vines, and letters, and I adopted these themes and elaborated on them.

    I frequently base my newer samplers on a composite theme, making the figures appear lifelike, though taking care not to overdo it so that they do not appear banal. The old samplers were usually worked on fine openwork material with many different colors, and I always retain these characteristics. Occasionally, however, I work a design on linen D, but the fine linen usually gives the best effect.

    The tiny faces of my first people were never given any expression, because there wasn't sufficient room, but as soon as I made the face bigger, using more stitches, it was tempting to put in an expression with the help of a few stitches, as, for example, in Fig. 2-1.

    After that, it was tempting to draw slightly bigger faces with one cross-stitch for the eye and one for the mouth—and then still bigger faces with several stitches for the eyes and mouth. But there comes a point where you have to stop, because if you make the features too big, the results can often be disastrous.

    I had no direct models for the figures and faces as I had when I drew the flowers. A few pictures illustrating how I draw them are to be found in Figs. 3-26 and 3-28. (See pp. 88 and 89.)

***Facing page,*** 2-1. Wall hanging, Hans Christian Andersen, L.N. 3608A.
Size: 9½" x 13¾".
Danish Flower Thread on linen II, bleached.
This embroidery can also be sewn on linen D, bleached, L.N. 3608B.
Size: 15¾" x 23½".
In the latter case it is worked in Danish Flower Thread using double thread.

The fairy tales depicted in Fig. 2-1 are:
Numskull Jack
Five Peas from a Pod
The Little Match Girl
The Sweethearts
Little Ida's Flowers
The Emperor's New Clothes

The Teapot
The Shepherdess and the Chimneysweep
The Ugly Duckling
The Tinderbox
The Steadfast Tin Soldier
The Little Mermaid

53

2-2. Doily of April: ducks and weeping willow (from *The Year's Cross-Stitch, 1960)*.
Doily size: 6" x 6".
Danish Flower Thread on linen II.

2-3. Doily, March: skipping girls (from *The Year's Cross-Stitch, 1962)*.
Actual size of doily: 5½" x 5½".
Danish Flower Thread on linen II, bleached.

For the calendar shown in Fig. 2-2 I drew 12 different kinds of birds and animal motifs, all in red, shade No. 86.

I drew 12 different motifs connected with the seasons in the Danish countryside for the calendar illustrated in Fig. 2-3. The motifs were in many colors, but the borders were all worked in blue, shade No. 227.

*At left,* 2-4. Detail, bellpull with blue birds, L.N. 2652.
The bellpull is 4" x 64½" and consists of 2 different motifs, repeated alternately so that there are 6 motifs in all. Each motif is 10⅜" long.
Danish Flower Thread on linen IA.

*Above,* 2-5. Mini bellpull with blue birds, L.N. 2928.
Size: 1¾" x 10".
Danish Flower Thread on linen II, bleached.

*Overleaf:* 2-6. Wall picture, "I will build myself a farm," L.N. 2782.
Size: 20" x 31".
Danish Flower Thread on linen D, bleached.

◇ I WILL BUILD

YSELF A FARM

2-7. Cushion for Father (from *The Children's Embroidery Book,* published in 1962 by the Danish Handcraft Guild).
Size: 13¾" x 13¾".
Danish Flower Thread on linen D, bleached.

The pattern above was inspired by an old Danish embroidery of the last century. It features, among other things, a small group of people (onlookers) with stiff, staring expressions. The embroidery is worked entirely in blues and grays.

The embroidery below is kept in one color, either blue No. 17 or red No. 86. A corresponding embroidery, girls' choir, L.N. 2735, is the same in size, quality, and color, but of course the figures are different.

2-8. Wall hanging, boys' choir, L.N. 2790.
Size: 6" x 7¾".
Danish Flower Thread on linen II, bleached.

59

2-9. Cushion for Mother (from *The Children's Embroidery Book*).
Size: 13¾" x 13¾".
Danish Flower Thread on linen D, bleached.

The cushion for Mother on this page is worked in the same blue and gray shades as the cushion for Father. Both patterns are easy to sew, and for this reason they were included in a handbook for children.

The motifs for the bookmarks come from the cushion for Father and the cushion for Mother and are seen here on 2 different linens—linen D, bleached, and linen II, bleached.

2-10. Bookmarks (from *The Children's Embroidery Book*).

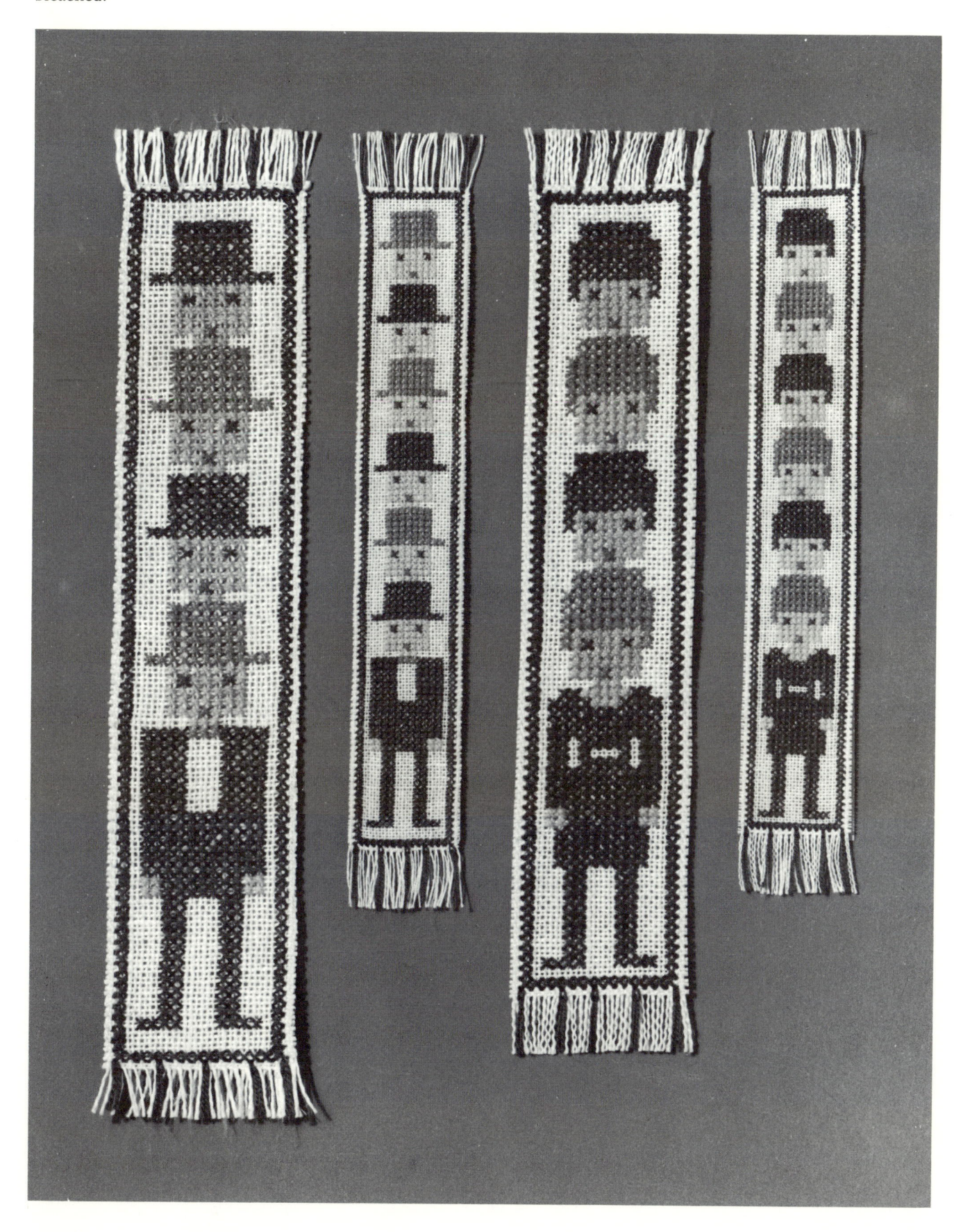

61

2-11. Cushion, schoolboys, L.N. 3158.
Size: 12¼" x 12½".
Danish Flower Thread, D.M.C., and Clark on linen Hanne.

The embroideries shown in Figs. 2-11 and 2-12 are drawn from a wall hanging for which I greatly enjoyed drawing 221 children's faces, all of them different. The best of the boys' faces were then arranged on the cushion shown in Fig. 2-11, and the girls' faces on the cushion in Fig. 2-12.

2-12. Cushion, schoolgirls, L.N. 3157.
Size: 12¼" x 12½".
Danish Flower Thread, D.M.C., and Clark on linen Hanne.

The cushion in Fig. 2-12 was sewn by an 8-year-old boy for our exhibition at the Danish Museum for Decorative Arts in 1966. To be sure, it is stitched on the coarsest embroidery linen in the book, but as it was necessary to thread the needle and manipulate several threads at a time, I must say he managed exceedingly well.

2-13. Wall hanging, song choir, L.N. 3627.
Size: 7" x 9".
Danish Flower Thread on linen II, bleached.

*Facing page,* 2-14. Diagram for wall hanging with song choir, L.N. 3627.
Watercolor on graph paper.
Cutting measurements: 10⅛" x 12¼".
Finished measurements: 7" x 9".
Danish Flower Thread on linen II, bleached, worked with single thread, shade No. 86.

For the wall hanging in Fig. 2-14, begin by working the border at a point 1⅝" in and down from the upper left-hand corner. Make the hem 13 threads wide.

65

*Chapter 3.*

# HOW TO DESIGN FOR CROSS-STITCH

A drawing intended to be used as a cross-stitch pattern must first be mapped out on design paper, i.e., graph paper. (See the graph paper illustrated in Fig. 3-1 and a description of the kinds of graph paper needed on p. 133.) Two threads of the material correspond to 1 square on the graph paper.

If you look at Fig. 3-1, you will see that:

A. By drawing over the horizontal and vertical lines of the squares, it is possible to trace the outline of the surface intended to be worked in cross-stitch.

B. Since 1 square on the graph paper is equal to 2 threads of the material, it is also possible to draw in the middle of the squares with horizontal and vertical lines. Single cross-stitches may then be shifted over by a single thread in relation to the remaining cross-stitches.

C. Oblong squares can be drawn both longitudinally and transversely. This type of stitch is called the half cross-stitch, and passes over 1 thread in one direction and 2 threads in the other.

D. Lines may be drawn diagonally from one corner of the square to the other, representing the backstitch passing over 2 threads. The backstitch passing over 2 threads can also be drawn vertically and horizontally.

E. For the backstitch in other directions, lines can also be drawn that move one whole square up, but only half a square sideways, or vice versa.

F. The backstitch can also be drawn diagonally, horizontally, and vertically, all such stitches passing over one thread or over a single intersection.

G. Stitches can be drawn as ¾ cross-stitches, passing diagonally over 2 threads or over a single intersection, respectively. (See, in addition, the stitch diagrams on page 124.)

3-1   A       B       C       D       E       F       G

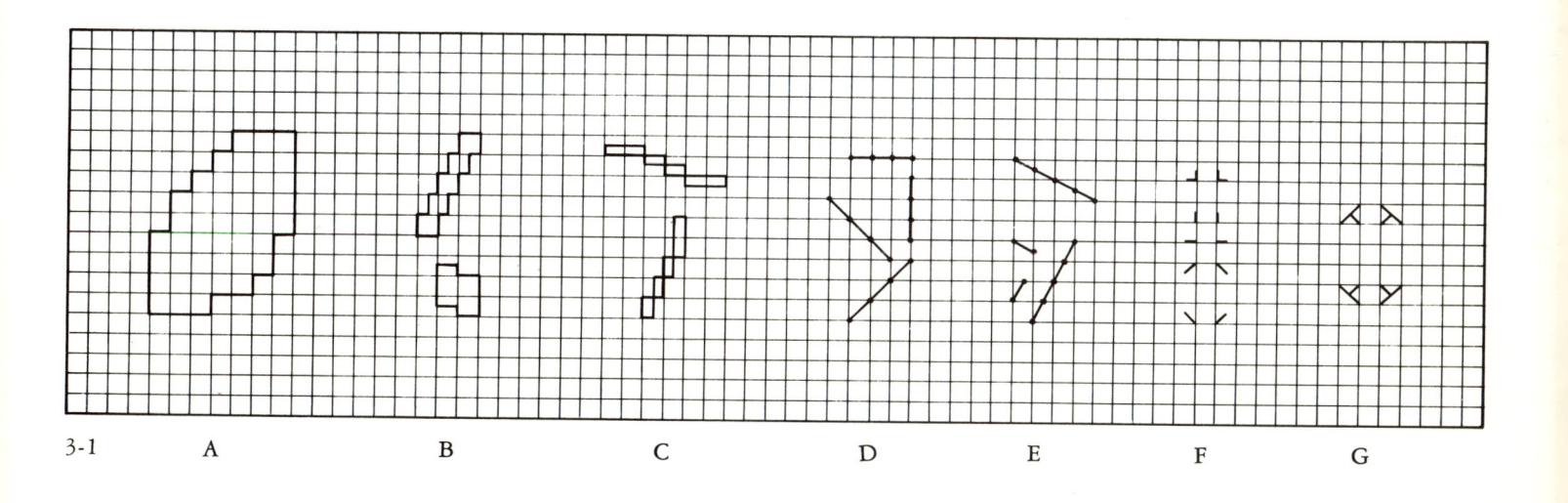

For all my cross-stitch patterns I use 2 kinds of paper:

1) Tracing paper 111¼ that I obtain from I. C. Petersen, in Copenhagen, and whose approximate equivalent can no doubt be gotten in other countries. This tracing paper is to be found in various qualities, but a firm texture is necessary, as the paper is first drawn on with pencil, after which all the superfluous lines have to be erased. This paper is unsuitable for painting. (See also p. 133.)

2) Graph paper, as mentioned before. There are numerous kinds of graph paper. When I draw a design for an embroidery on coarse linen, I use paper with big squares, and if the embroidery is to be on fine linen, I choose paper with smaller squares.

3-2    A1           A2           A3           B1           B2

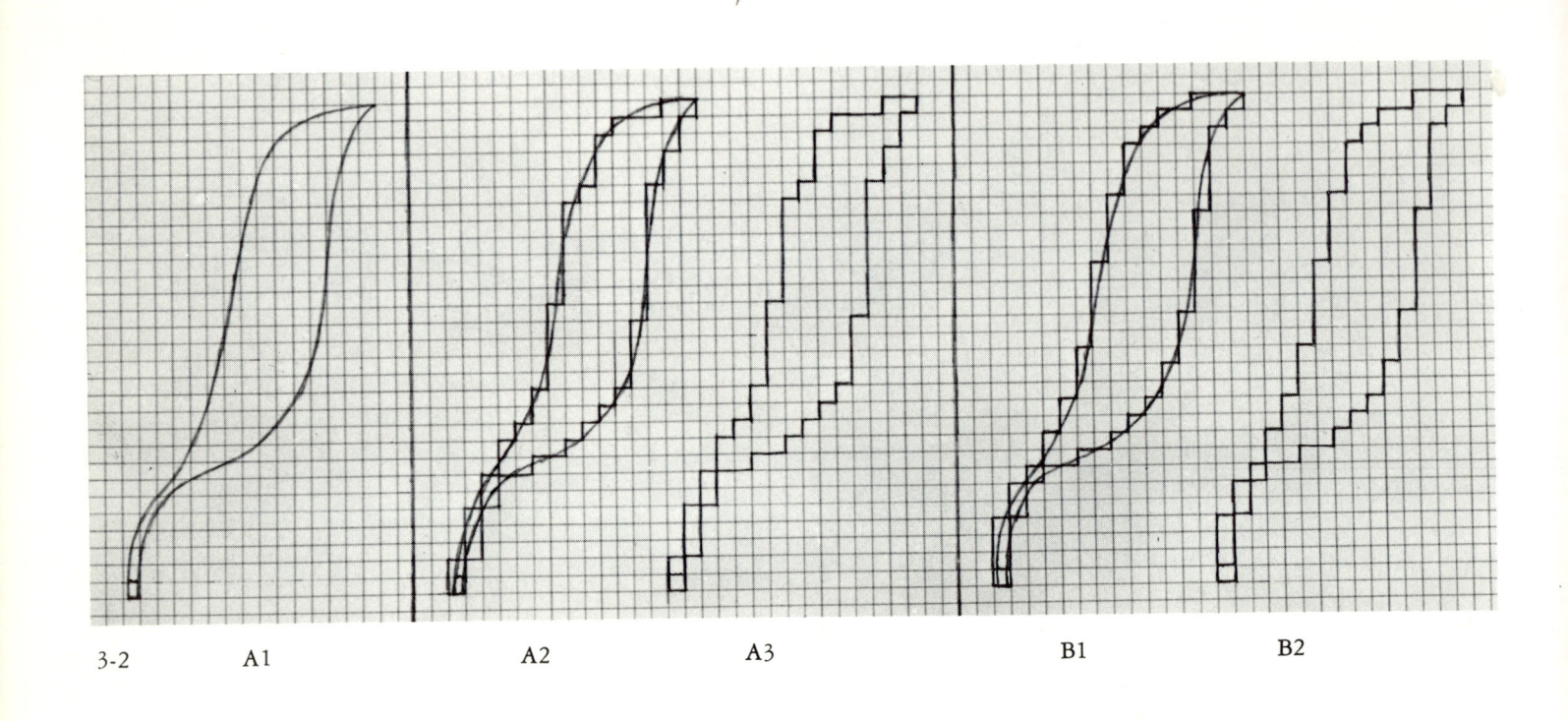

For the above drawing I have laid the tracing paper on top of the graph paper, and fixed both firmly to the drawing board by means of thumbtacks. I do not draw directly onto the graph paper because its fine lines are liable to be rubbed off. Fig. 3-2 represents an example of my procedure in drawing a design, as follows:

A1) First, a leaf to be worked in cross-stitch is drawn in outline.
A2) The same outline as before is shown, but it is now a question of following the outline as closely as possible by means of vertical and horizontal lines.
A3) This I call a working drawing. The angular lines from A2 have been copied, omitting the outline. However, since the result is not good, the process must be repeated.
B1) The outline is shown again, but with a slightly different interpretation.
B2) Now the working drawing reveals a better result—I hope so at any rate, for in A2 I did my utmost to create a bad one!

The conversion of line to squares is like so much else—a matter of practice. The following various exercises might be studied and further developed by beginners.

# LINES IN CROSS-STITCH

Before trying more difficult cross-stitch patterns, I would recommend practicing the drawing of very simple cross-stitch lines, as in the few examples given in Fig. 3-3.

In all 3 designs of this figure, the 4 stages of the line are illustrated: a. the given line; b. the given line and its equivalent in squares; c. the working drawing alone; and d. the cross-stitch line.

With straight lines, as in drawings 1, 2, and 3, the gradations are seen to rise evenly, and this applies to all other straight lines, of whatever gradient. Drawings 4 and 5 represent a curved line and a curved line with indentation, respectively. For circles of all sizes I always use a compass and draw in the radius and diameter, as shown.

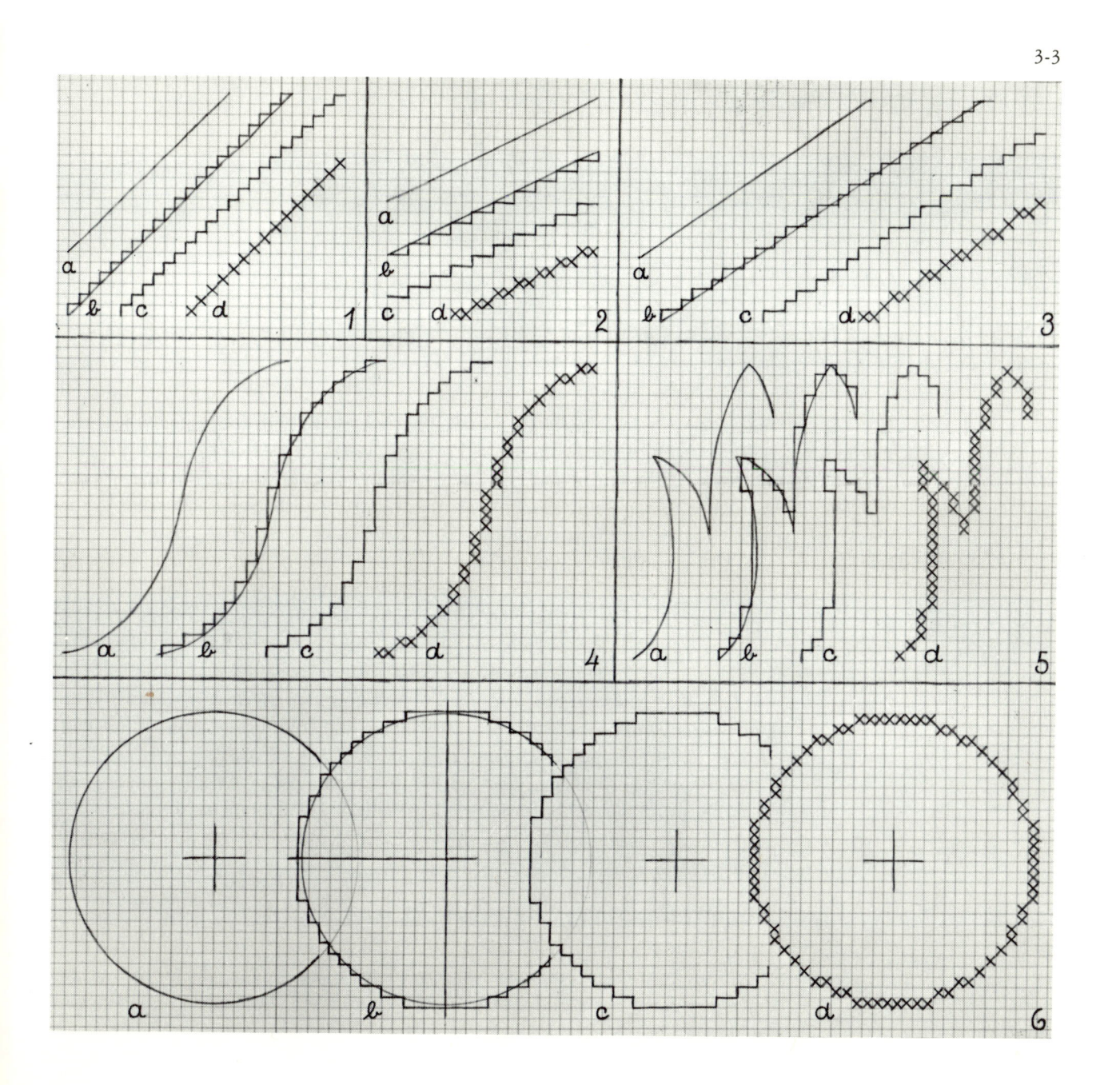

3-3

69

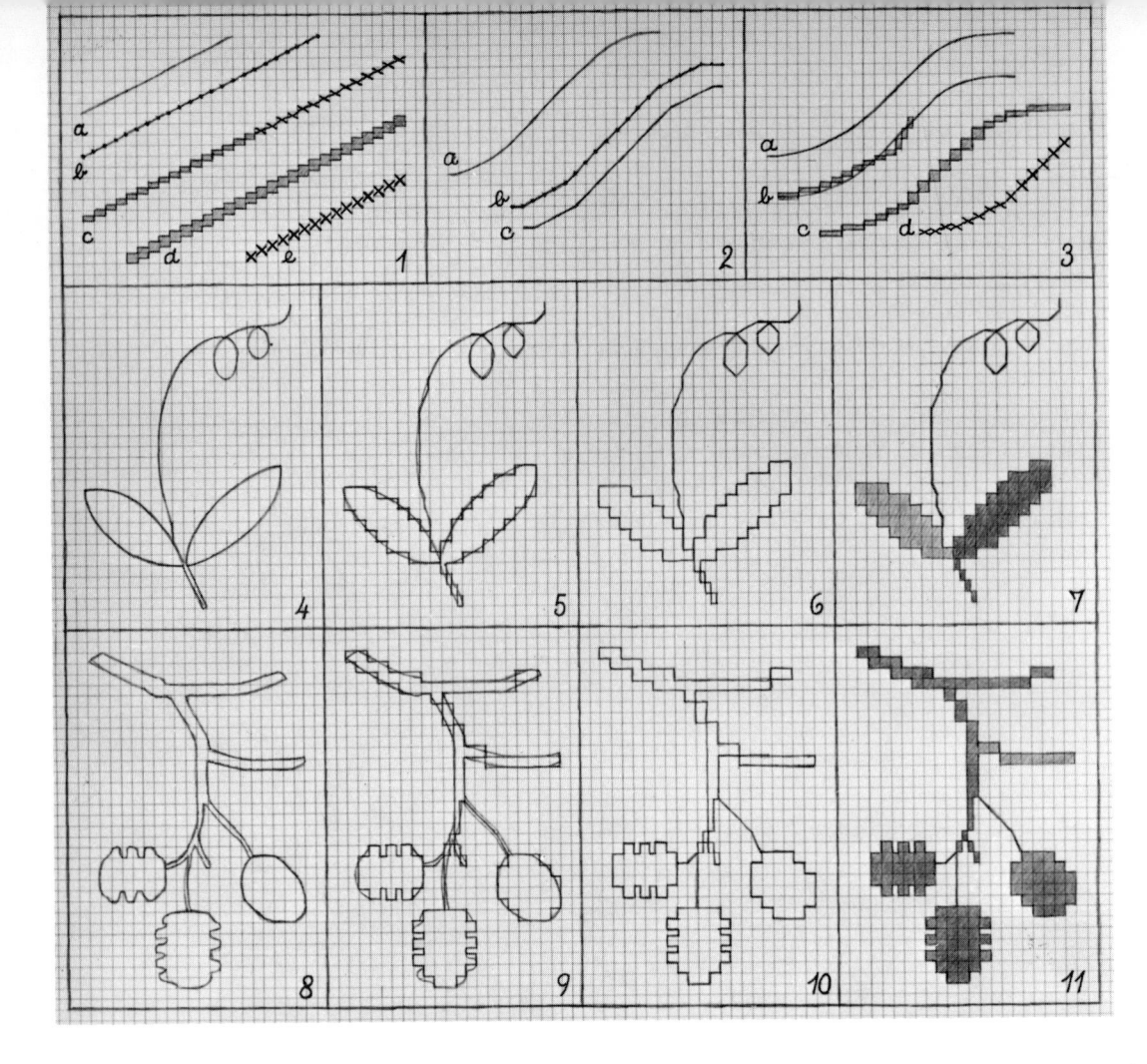

3-4. Drawing a variety of stitches on graph paper.

## LINES AND MOTIFS WITH VARIOUS OTHER STITCHES

In Fig. 3-4, note:

1a. The given line; b. the line worked in backstitch, with the points where the needle pierces the material being marked by dots; c. the same line worked with half cross-stitches, and the last half of the line drawn in cross-stitches; d. the line worked in cross-stitches that are shifted over by a single thread; e. the same cross-stitch line as it looks when drawn in cross-stitches.

2a. The given line; b. the line worked in cross-stitch. The needle holes are indicated by a dotted line; c. a working drawing of the same line without dots.

3a. The given line; b. this line cannot be drawn entirely in half cross-stitches without going off the track; c. the same line can only be worked out with the aid of whole cross-stitches; d. the lower part of "c" drawn in cross-stitches.

4, 5, 6, and 7. The motif is a detail of the everlasting pea drawn in 4 stages. The thinnest line is drawn in backstitches, whereas the stalk below is drawn in half cross-stitches and the leaves in whole cross-stitches.

8, 9, 10, and 11. This motif consists of details of alder drawn in 4 stages. The thinnest twigs are drawn in backstitches, a couple of small branches in half cross-stitches, with a few cross-stitches in a shifted pattern on the catkins, and the rest in whole cross-stitches.

## INSTRUCTIONS FOR DRAWING PATTERNS

1. Every time I start on a new pattern I have at least one model in front of me. As I have previously mentioned, these may vary greatly. The model or models that serve as the first inspiration I call step 1.

2. I place the graph paper on the drawing board, cover it with tracing paper, and fasten the two sheets at the 4 corners with thumbtacks, for it is very important that they do not become detached from one another during the work. On the chosen material I have already counted out how many threads I may use for my pattern in either direction. As stated before, 2 threads on the material are equal to one square on the paper. I mark the number of stitches on the tracing paper, through which I can easily see the squares. Then I may begin the drawing itself, which must be a line drawing, not yet converted to the horizontal and vertical lines that make up the squares. In the end, the drawing must be clear-cut and precise, with any rough sketched-in lines erased. The drawing of the squares is the next step.

3. Still using the same drawing, I now begin to follow the contours of the line drawing with horizontal and vertical lines, and I make sure I follow the line as closely as possible and that all the spatial units so produced are well formed. This drawing always consists, in the end, of 2 lines—a smooth line and an angular one.

4. Now I take another piece of graph paper of the same size and quality as the first. I lay it by the side of my drawing, and copy directly onto this graph paper the angular lines from the previous step, omitting, however, the original line drawing. This is accomplished simply, by means of counting.

I now have my working drawing, which may also be obtained by another method:

Instead of taking a fresh sheet of graph paper, I release the tracing paper along its bottom edge, at the same time making sure that the two pieces of paper are firmly held together at the top. Then I transfer a few horizontal and vertical lines at a time onto the graph paper beneath, constantly replacing the tracing paper in order to check that the marked-off lines lie in the right place.

For the practiced draftsman the latter is the quicker method, but my pupils always prefer the first one. When the working drawing is finished, I take out my shade card and decide which colors I am going to sew with. I note the shade number in pencil in several of the areas. Where dark colors are to be used, I shade the area lightly in pencil, because this prevents the drawing from getting too confusing. Now and again I also decide to give some of the pattern depth, by using light and medium tones, and shadow effects. Here, too, shading is useful—light shading for the medium values and darker penciling-in for the shadows. Then I start to paint the drawing.

5. I always use watercolors (never colored pencils) for this next step. Every time I mix a new color, I apply a small sample to the graph paper and compare it with the thread number on the shade card. I nearly always paint the dark colors over twice; otherwise they are not dark enough. In the margin of the drawing, I pick out small squares in which I note the shade number of every color to be used. I always try to make the painted drawing resemble the envisaged embroidery as closely as possible. Only then do I let it go out for sewing.

6. The material should now lie ready. with the threads already counted out. I know the precise area to be covered. If it should happen that parts of the finished embroidery do not come up to expectation, they will have to be undone and something better worked out. The mounting of the embroidery is then finally decided upon and tried out.

These 6 stages of my procedure will now be illustrated as, in the following pages, I shall demonstrate how they apply to some of my embroideries.

3-5. Step 1.

3-6. Step 2.

## EXERCISE WITH 3 PRESSED LEAVES

Shown in the first step are, from the top downwards on the left, leaves of sweetbrier, red currant, and Virginia creeper, which form the models.

In the second step, the line drawing is begun.

72

3-7. Step 3.

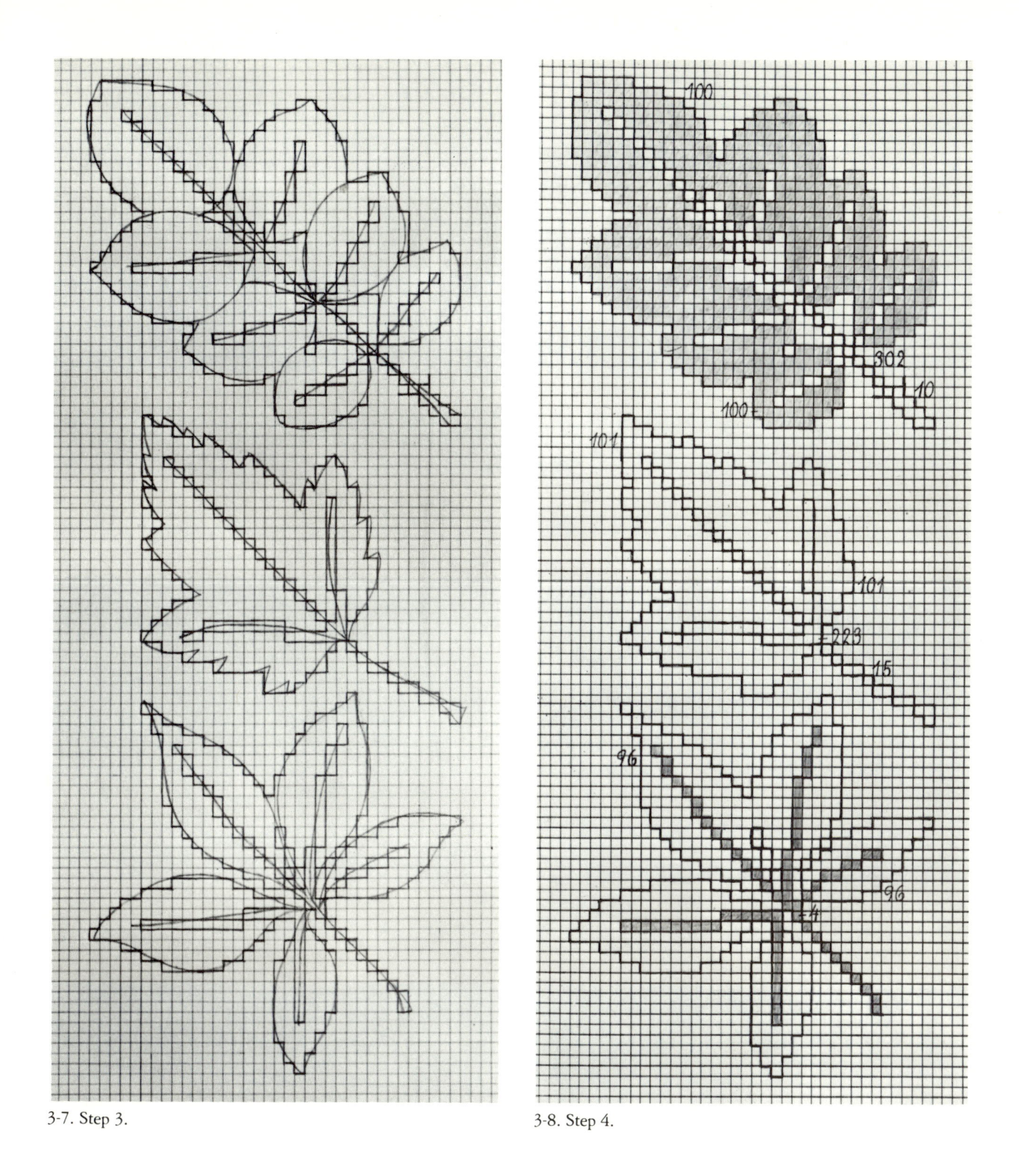

3-8. Step 4.

In the third step, the outline of vertical and horizontal lines is superimposed on the smooth line.

Then, with the omission of the smooth outline, the working drawing is obtained (3-8).

73

3-9. Step 5.

3-10. Step 6.

In the fifth step, I apply the watercolor to areas in the working design, noting on the bottom the shade numbers of the colors I've used. The final step (3-10) shows the embroidered work on canvas 10.5 with Danish Flower Thread.

# REPEATING PATTERNS FOR TABLECLOTH WITH IVY

When I drew this pattern especially for this book, my idea was to draw two vines down the middle of a tablecloth (see Fig. 3-11). The pattern had to be a repeating pattern and to fit into one page of the book.

    First I picked a vine of ivy and a few separate leaves, and I laid them between 2 newspapers with some heavy books on top. The newspapers were changed every few days and in about 8 to 10 days the vine and the leaves were dry enough to be stuck onto white cardboard, which I did with transparent tape that doesn't become brown with age. There is a special kind of paper that can be used for pressing plants, but I find that newspapers are equally good for this purpose and are, moreover, always available.

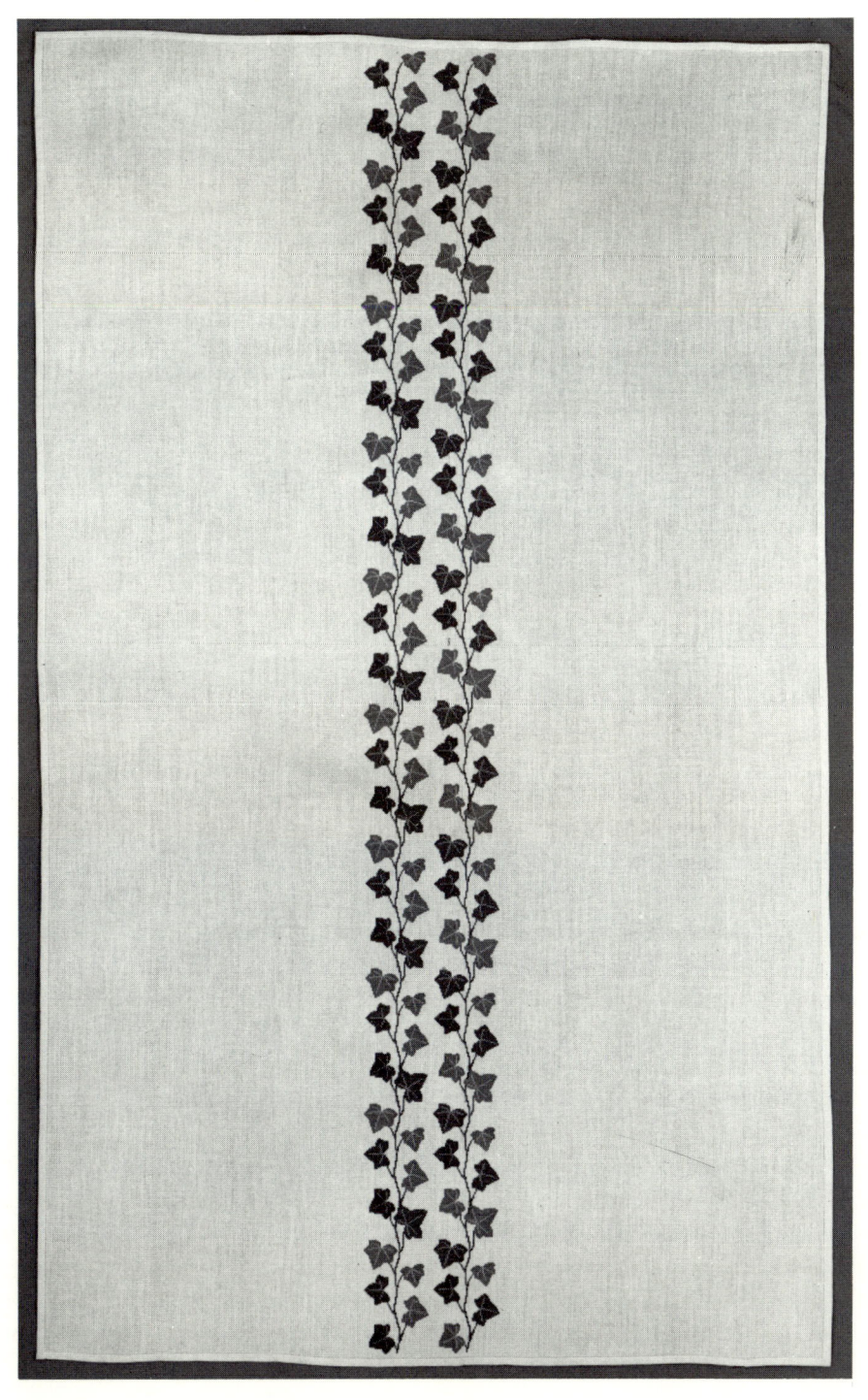

3-11

3-12. Ivy *(Hedera helix)*. Step 1: the pressed plant as model.

Since I wanted the tablecloth to be of linen IA, I counted out how many stitches I had available for the repeat in each direction. It was 104 x 104 stitches, and this I marked out on the paper (remembering that 1 square equals 2 threads of the linen). I couldn't use the whole page, for I had to leave room for the repeats.

First I drew the leaf AI in the left-hand vine (see Fig. 3-13), and then I repeated it vertically for 104 squares below. The next leaf, AII, marked the beginning of the second repeat. After that I drew leaf BI, still in the left-hand vine, and repeated it vertically for 104 stitches below. Next, I started on the right-hand vine, repeating leaves AI and BI in the same way, and thereafter drawing the second repeats, AII and BII, vertically below.

Only now could the composition proper begin, for I had fixed the limits within which I might draw. The two vines were to be identical, and designed so as to form a whole. The transition from one repeat to the other had to be tried out and appear natural, almost accidentally arrived at. It took me several attempts to come up with the final version, and the rough sketches were then erased in order to leave only one precise line. During the whole process I kept the model of the first step in mind, though I was unable to follow it exactly (see Fig. 3-12).

3-13. Step 2: the line drawing.

In the third stage, I continued to draw on the paper used in Step 2, superimposing the horizontal and vertical lines now. I tried to make sure that the leaves were well-shaped and that the stems appeared thin in some places and thicker in others. Since the vines were to be identical, it was sufficient to confine this procedure to only one of them.

3-14. Step 3.

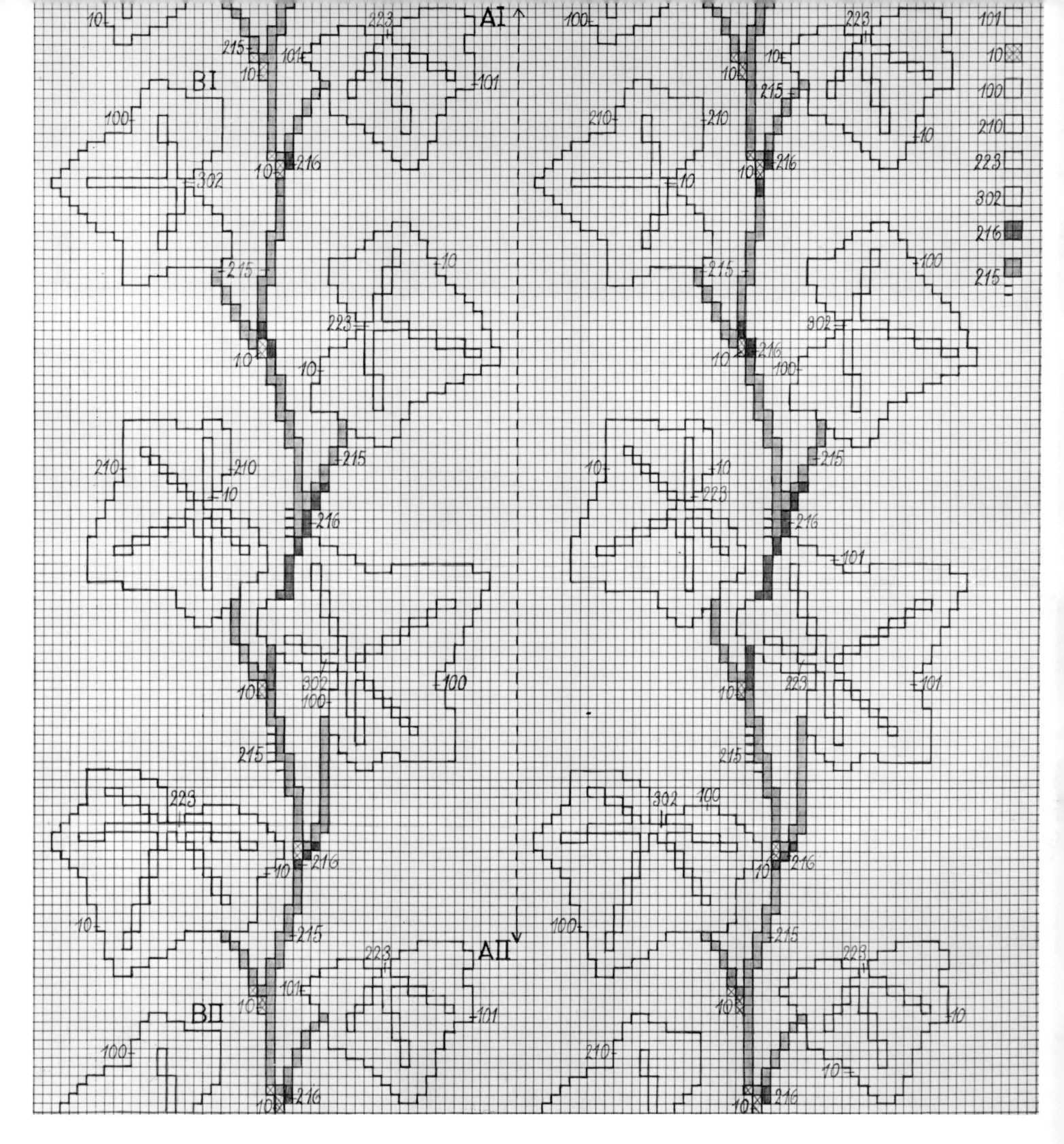

To get the working drawing—the fourth stage—I took a fresh sheet of paper and copied Step 3 twice, but omitting the lines from Step 2. (See Fig. 3-15.) This time I added a few air roots (it is always best to leave the details until a later stage).

The two vines were identical with regard to line, but I didn't wish them to be identical in color. I brought out the shade card and penciled in the thread numbers on every color area. On the right-hand side I charted the shade numbers.

I shaded the stems in lightly with a pencil. (The dotted lines mark the middle of the drawing and also give the number of stitches in one repeat: 104 stitches.)

3-15. Step 4: the working drawing.

79

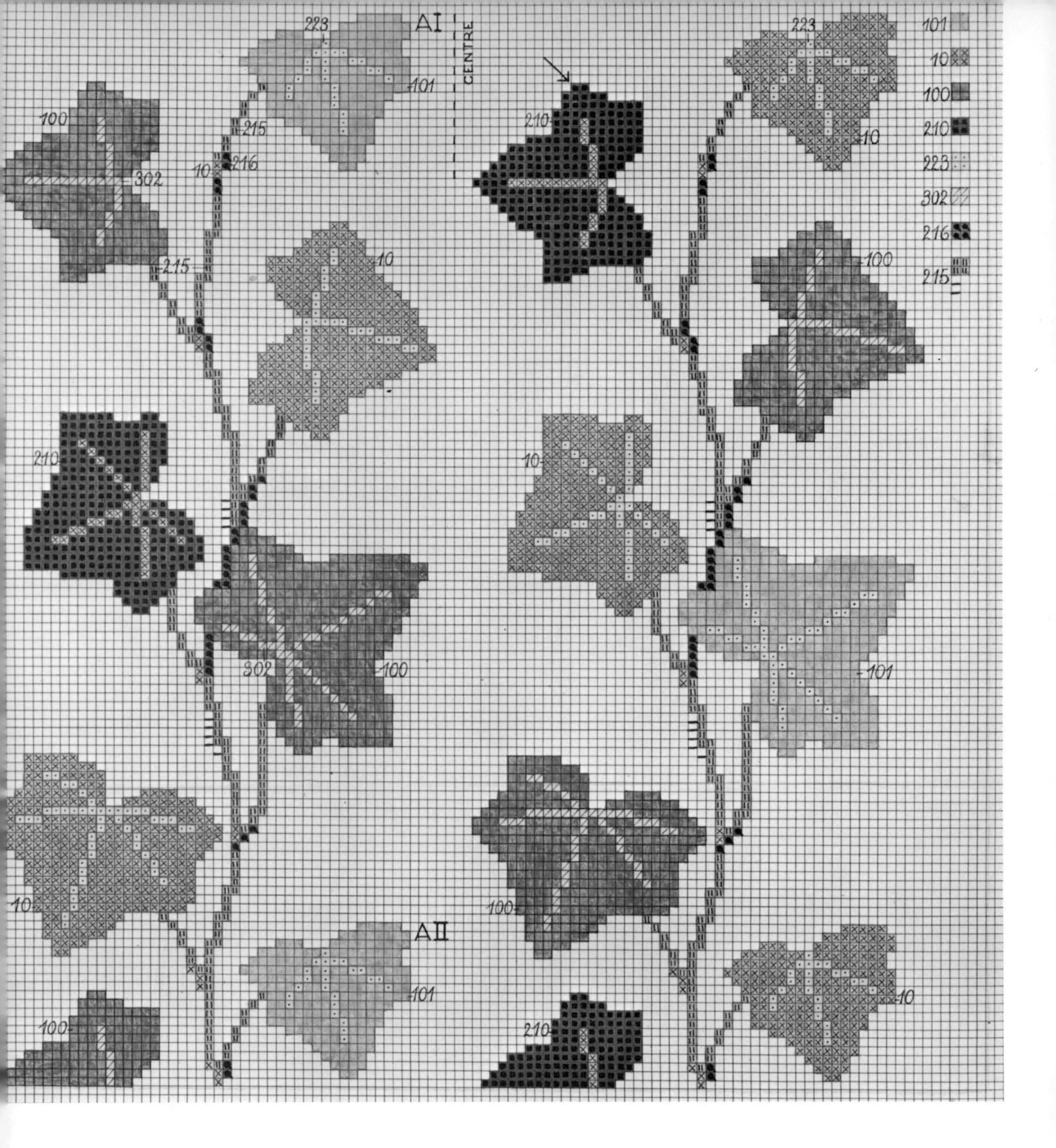

3-16. Step 5: the drawing in color.

Now, for the fifth stage, out came the watercolors. I began with the light green shades, then the middle greens, and finally the dark greens and browns. I painted the dark areas twice in order to make them dark enough. Anyone wanting to embroider this pattern should note that I inserted symbols with India ink in some of the color areas. In this way I avoided having too many numbers and I also rubbed out most of the midline, so that the total effect would not be spoiled.

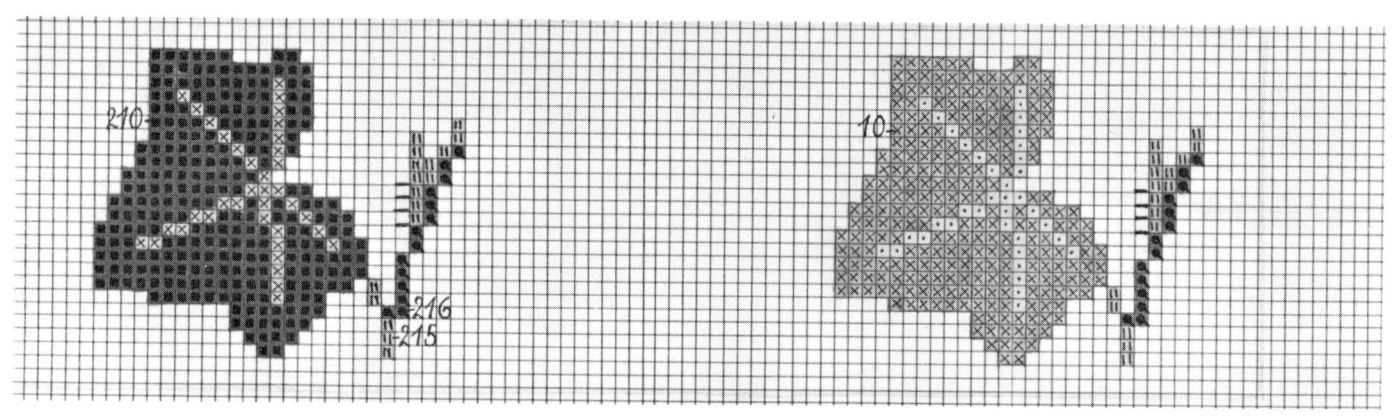

3-17. The end of the ivy tablecloth embroidery.

3-18. The right side of the upper left-hand vine.

3-19. The reverse side of the same piece of the vine embroidery.

The most important change when compared with the previous step was in the top part of the drawing. I did not wish the embroidery to begin in such an abrupt manner, so I altered that part of the embroidery.

When first picking up the material to do the embroidery, find the middle of the 44" side of the linen. Measure 5" down and count 26 threads to the right. This corresponds to the arrow on the pattern. (See Fig. 3-16.) Start the embroidery here, remembering as always that one square on the pattern is equal to two threads of linen.

Work the repeat indicated from AI to AII 9 times. Start working the 10th repeat, but finish it as shown in Fig. 3-17.

The final data about this embroidery are:

Ivy table cloth, L.N. 3592.
Size: 40" x 69".
Cutting measurements: 44¼" x 76½".
Thread: Danish Flower Thread, single thread.
Material: Linen IA.
Technique: 13 threads-wide hem, the hem stitch passing over 3 threads. (For hem-stitch instructions, see p. 126.)

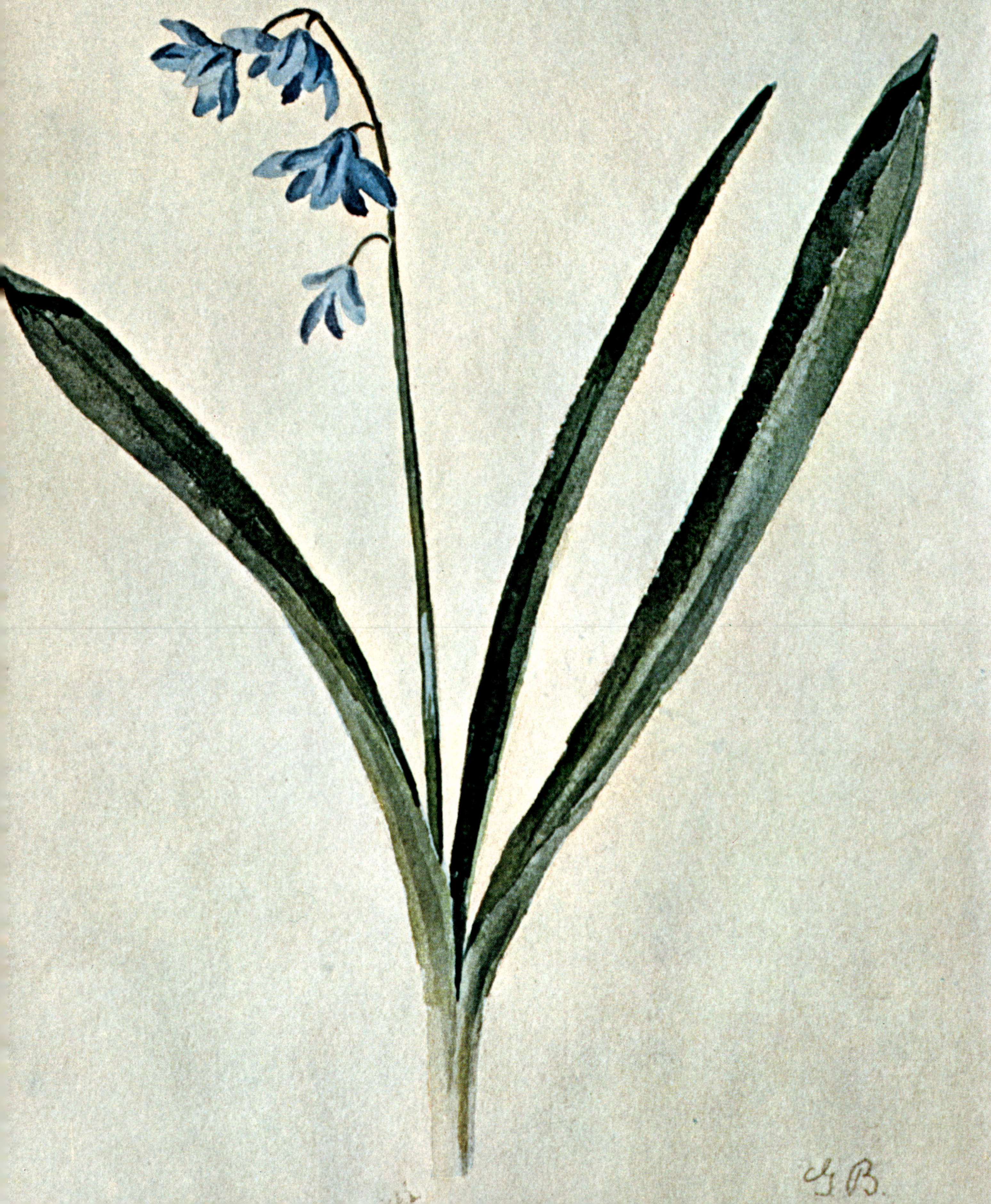
G.B.

## PATTERN FOR DOILY WITH SCILLA

I picked the scilla in my garden one day. I was to use it two weeks later as the model for a pattern forming part of a particular series, in which all the flowers were 70 stitches high and 70 stitches wide. When I counted out the number of stitches on paper and drew the square within which the pattern was to be composed, I very soon discovered I had to have another flower. Luckily they had not yet faded.

As you will see, you cannot always count on your own model being sufficient.

As may be seen, at this stage I found it advisable to also use some cross-stitches in a shifting pattern, half cross-stitches, and backstitches, chiefly on account of the flowers' very thin and slender stalks.

*Facing page:* 3-20. Step 1: a watercolor of the herb scilla.

*Above,* 3-21. Step 2: the line drawing for a pattern with scilla.

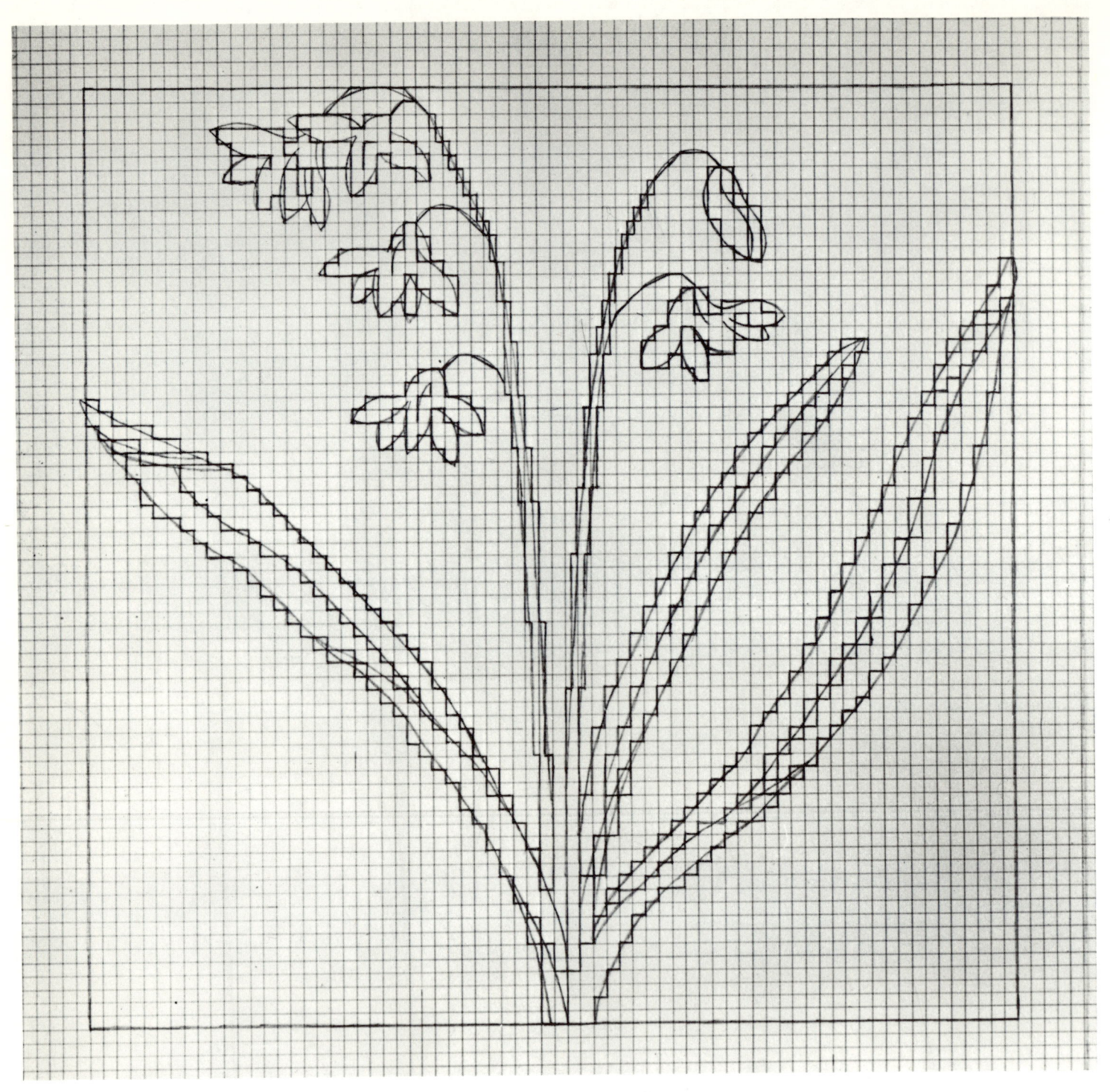

3-22. Step 3: drawing the vertical and horizontal lines over the smooth line.

84

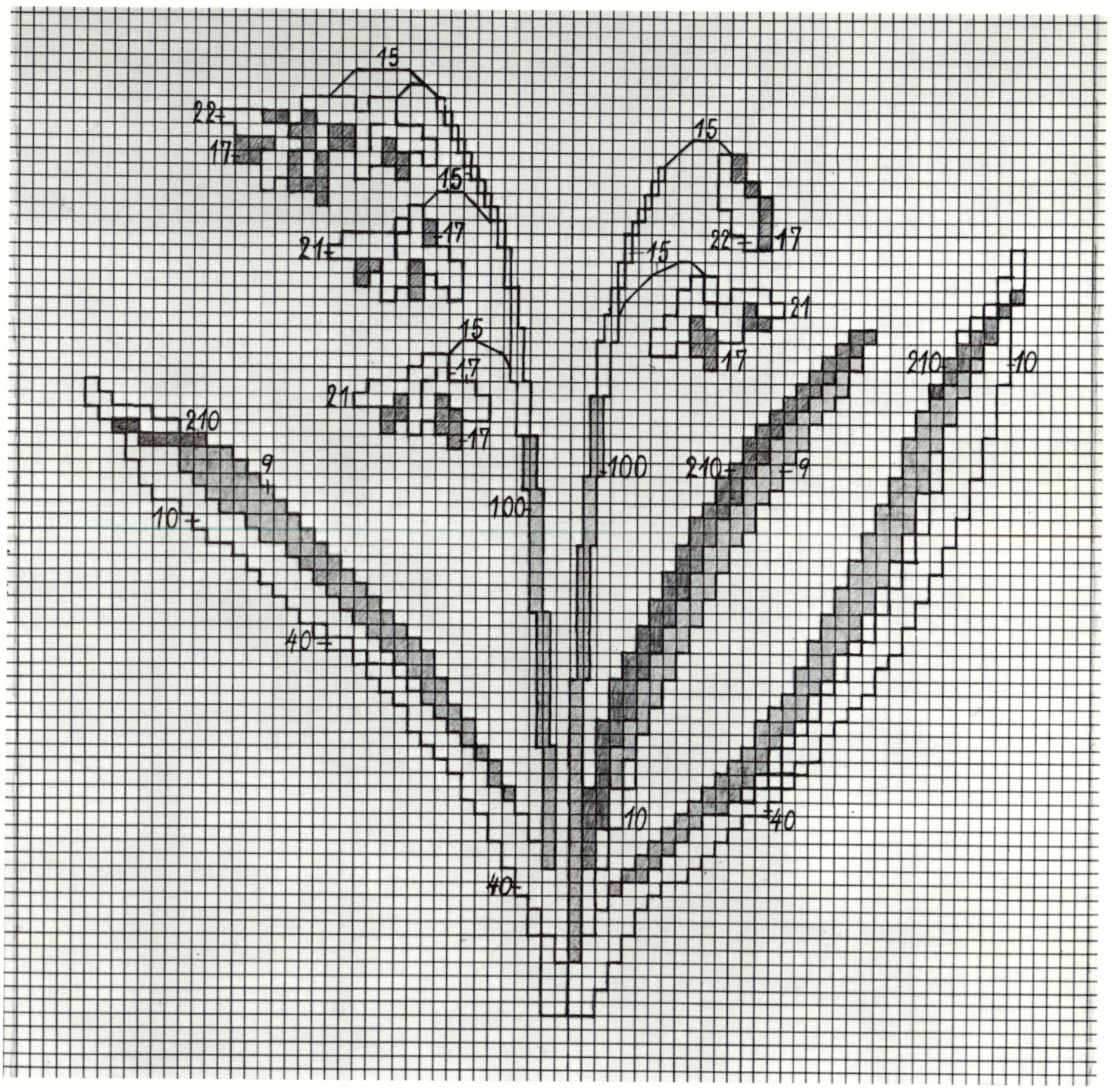

3-23. Step 4: the working drawing of the scilla.

Not until you have gotten rid of the first smooth-line drawing can you judge how successful you have been with the outline of squares. If I am satisfied with it, then I take out my shade card and give all the separate areas a thread number. I shade the dark areas in lightly with pencil.

85

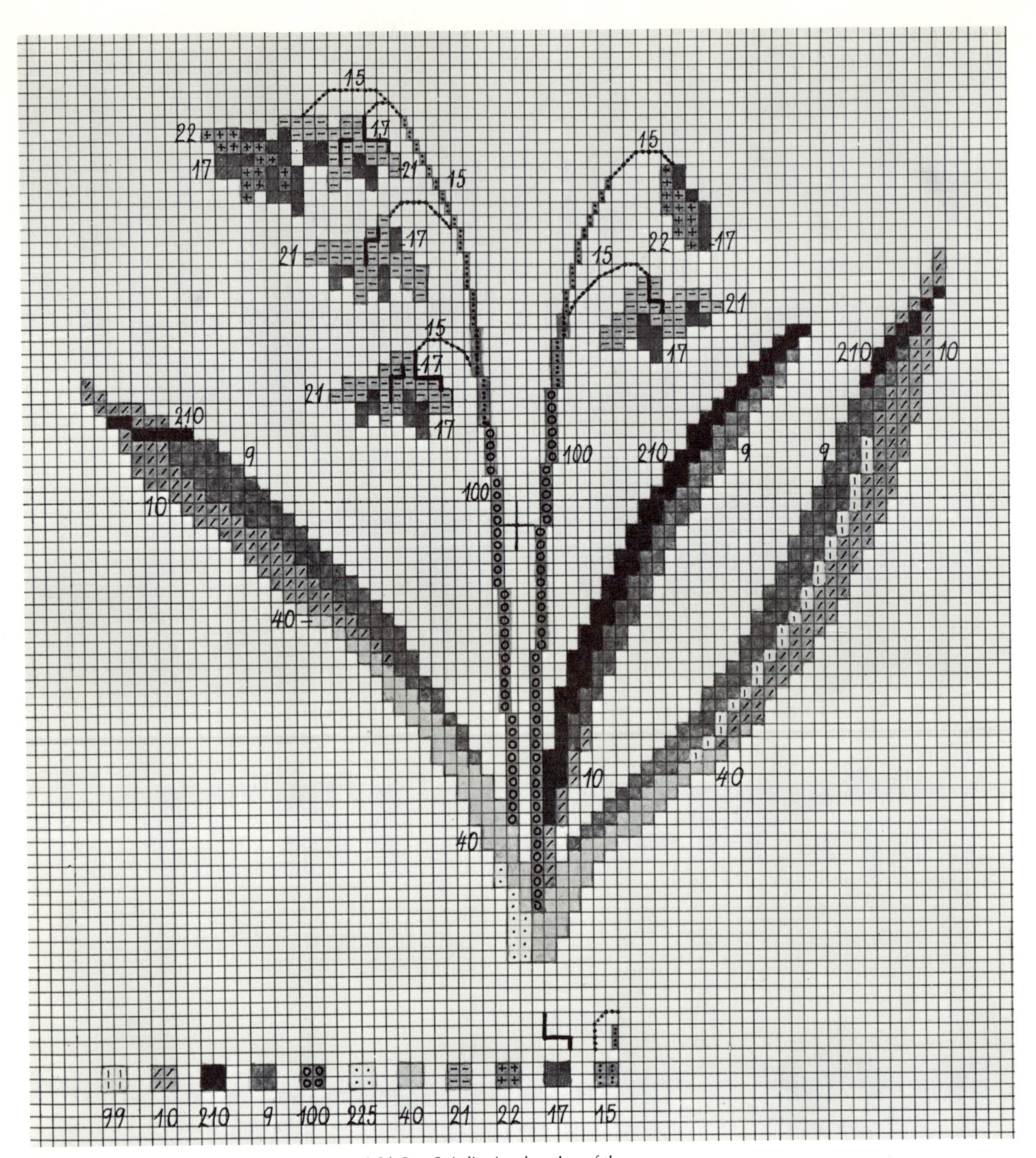

3-24. Step 5: indicating the colors of the threads.

86

3-25. Doily, scilla, L.N. 1965.
Size: 6" x 6".
Cutting measurement: 7½" x 7½".
Danish Flower Thread on linen I, hemmed,
using a hemstitch passing over 3 threads.
Hem: 7 threads wide.

Since the scilla pattern is not painted in, the colors are not shown, and so I have put a few symbols on some of the areas. A center cross is added to the drawing, corresponding to the midpoint of the piece of material now lying ready for counting out, and the embroidery is begun from this point. The finished result is seen in Fig. 3-25.

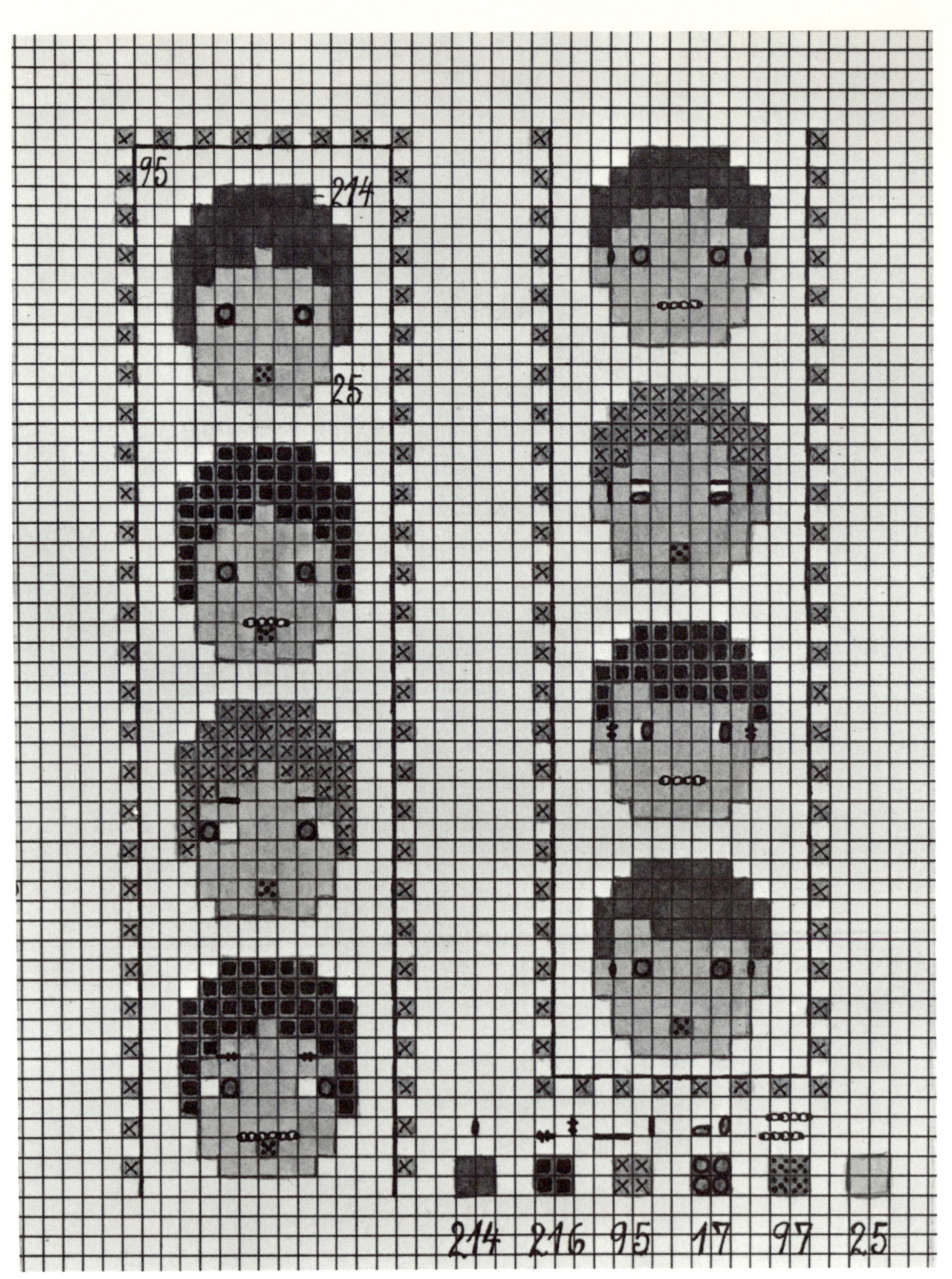

3-26. The thread colors are indicated for the bellpull shown in Fig. 3-27.

3-27. Cross-stitch pattern for mini bellpull, children, L.N. 3603.
Size: 1¾" x 11¾".
Cutting measurements: 2 pieces, 4¼" x 14⅛".
Thread: Danish Flower Thread, embroidered with 2 threads.
Material: Linen D, bleached.

3-28. Faces and figures in cross-stitch and backstitch.

For the embroidery in Fig. 3-27, I used cross-stitches, backstitches, and half cross-stitches. To find where to begin the embroidery, measure a point on the material in the upper left-hand corner 1½" in and 1¼" down, which corresponds to the border's top left-hand stitch. To mount the embroidery, 2 threads from it are folded under on all 4 sides of the material. The accessories (hanging bar and finial that are both 2" wide) are sewn on above and below and fastened with small backstitches. The backing is cut to the exact size of the front piece and sewn on all the way round.

I do not always draw faces and figures in outline first, often drawing the smaller details in cross-stitch at once, without any models. In Fig. 3-28, note the different faces: 1. A child's face in 3 stages. First the number of cross-stitches for the eyes and mouth is determined; then comes the outline. 2 and 3 are the same face, but with a few variations. 4. A smaller face with a top hat, in three stages. 5. A girl's face in 3 stages. 6. A variation on No. five. 7. Two boys' faces—same head, but with different facial expressions. 8. A variation on No. seven. 9. A square of 16 stitches, within which both man and wife have been given some expression. 10. A square of 9 stitches, within which the man and wife have been given a little expression, using the backstitch. 11. A square of 9 stitches for the faces of the man and wife. 12. A rectangle of 6 stitches for the faces of the pixies. 13. A square of 4 stitches for each of the faces of 3 little men, but now there are no facial expressions. 14. Just 3 stitches can be used for a man seen in profile. 15. A square for the faces of 3 little men. 16. A square for the faces of 4 little soldiers. 17. A square for the faces of 2 little gymnasts. 18. A square for the faces of 3 dancing girls. One thread separates face and body.

89

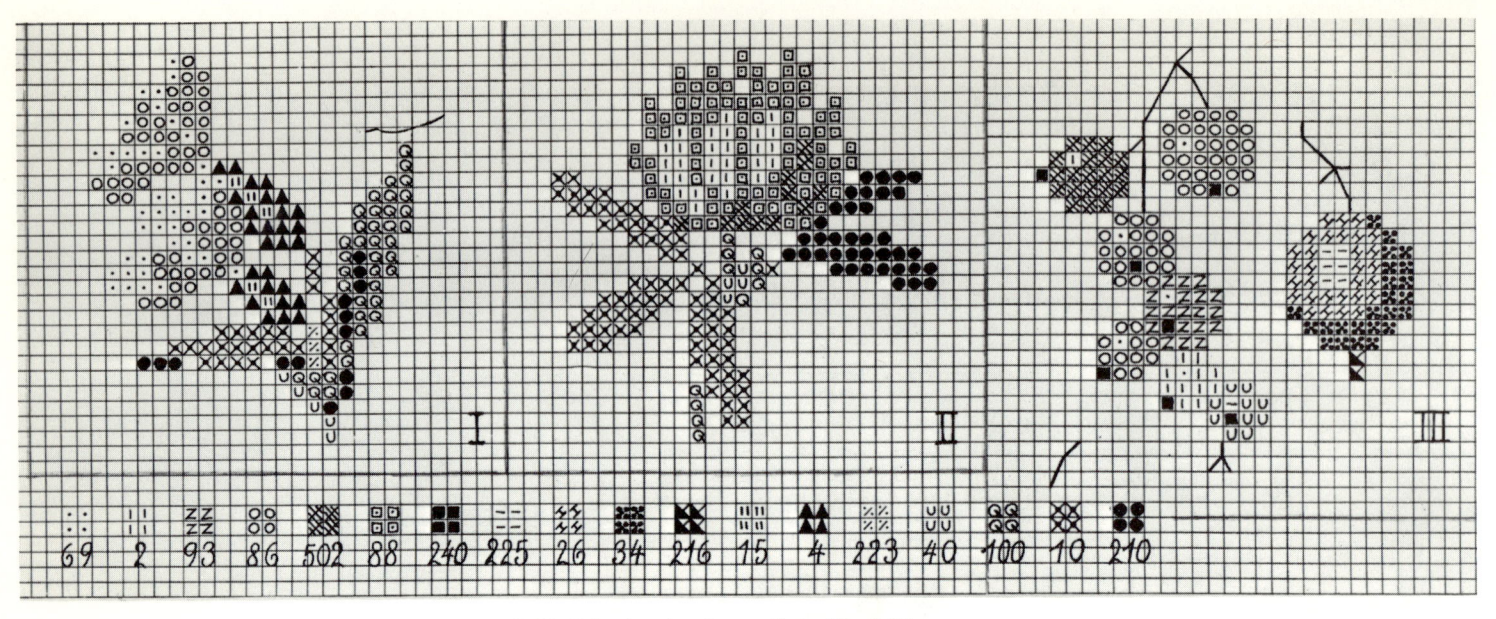

3-29. Color key for the motifs in Fig. 3-30.

In Fig. 3-29 every color has its own symbol. The pale shades have a pale symbol, the medium shades a slightly darker and heavier-looking symbol, and the dark colors the darkest and heaviest symbol.

I keep the leaves on my plants flat, without giving them any 3-dimensional effect. The fact that some leaves are darker than others, however, provides the plant with some perspective, so that some leaves appear to lie in front and others behind.

I treat flowers and fruit differently, using pale tones, medium tones, and shadows, so that even very small motifs appear 3-dimensional.

At the top of Fig. 3-30, on the left-hand side, the flower is seen in perspective, the effect being achieved by using a dark shade for the petals in the foreground and a light shade for those lying behind. Two colors are sufficient in this case. The calyx appears slightly rounded with the aid of a couple of lighter stitches in the middle.

The red currant fruits on the bottom row attain their globular form with the aid of only one stitch—a highlight placed a little to the left of each berry. The color used for the highlight varies according to the type of fruit.

With 3 different colors, the bigger gooseberry is given an oblong highlight, medium tones, and shadows—all determined by the gooseberry's oblong form.

The stages depicted below are:
- First stage: watercolor on drawing paper.
- Second stage: the cross-stitch pattern in watercolor on graph paper.
- Third stage: the motifs embroidered on linen II.

The flowers and fruits shown are, on top, red campion; in the middle, clover; and below, red currants and a gooseberry.

3-30. Flowers and fruits in 3 stages.

# Chapter 4.
# PAPER CUTOUTS FOR CROSS-STITCH DESIGNING

For the inexperienced designer I recommend cutting out the motifs in paper, since many pupils find this easier than drawing. With paper cutouts, there is the advantage that pupils are not tempted to go into too much detail in the beginning. It is better to consider the effect as a whole at first, leaving consideration of details for the time when the motifs are converted into embroidery patterns.

Something I always have my pupils do is to fold a piece of white paper in half, after which they are to cut out a figure resembling half a tulip. First of all I show them what half a tulip looks like and then I remove it from view. This experiment has always proved that a class of 12 different pupils will be sure to produce 12 different tulips—some thick and clumsy and others slim and elegant. For the results, look at the top row of Fig. 4-1. The middle row illustrates a different task. The paper was folded as before, but this time the students were to cut out their own motif. Now they really began to enjoy themselves; there was no shortage of ideas, and some of the results looked like this knapweed.

Clearly, motifs obtained by folding the paper in this fashion will always be symmetrical, but a different effect was achieved in the third exercise: setting one of their best motifs on the table, they used it as a model for a similar motif, but this time without folding the paper, so that a slight variation came about. This I call a free cutout.

The best motifs were then placed on the drawing board, covered with a piece of tracing paper, and the outlines were then drawn and either transferred straight onto material or onto graph paper, for converting into cross-stitch patterns.

So far, I have only described paper cutouts that are folded once, but a great variety of patterns can be gotten by folding the paper several different ways. Not only was Hans Christian Andersen an incomparable artist in this field, but many beautiful patterns also come from Poland, where they have always used brightly colored paper for their cutouts.

4-1

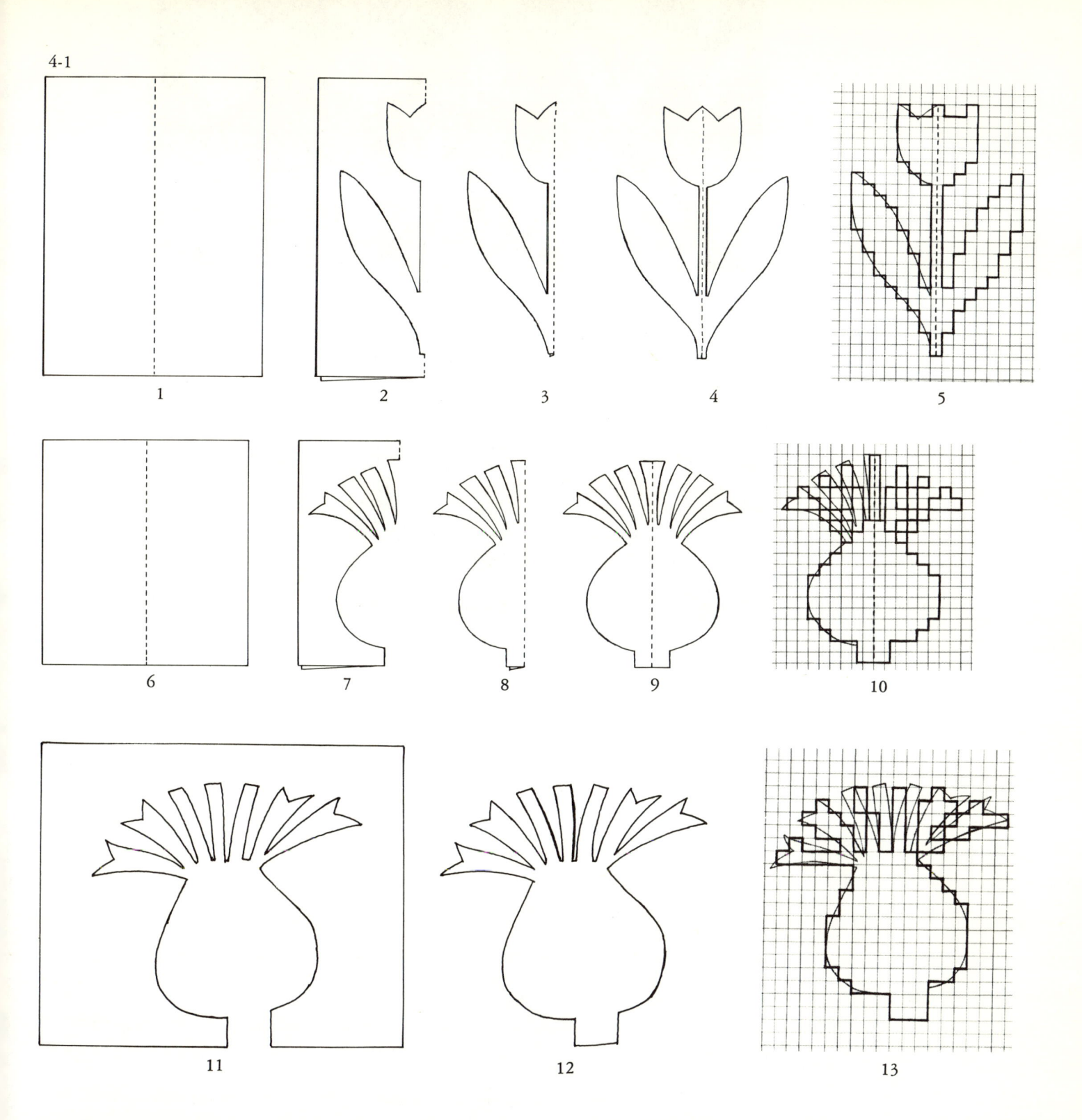

In Fig. 4-1, note the following steps:
  1. The paper is folded along the dotted line. 2. The motif is cut out. 3. The motif is folded over once. 4. Then it is spread out. 5. The motif, with smooth outline and squared outline that have been drawn on the tracing paper that covers the graph paper. 6. The paper is folded along the dotted line. 7. The motif is cut out. 8. The motif folded over once. 9. Then it is spread out. 10. The smooth outline and square outline of the motif as drawn on tracing paper that covers the graph paper. 11. The motif is cut out. 12. The motif is laid out. 13. The outlines of the motif on the tracing paper that covers the graph paper.

93

4-2. Paper cutouts on blue cardboard.

My pupils' paper cutouts were always mounted on blue cardboard, as shown above, for example, but slightly bigger and with a greater number of motifs on it. The obligatory tulip motif was placed on the extreme left, and thereafter came the students' own compositions—symmetrical and asymmetrical ones side by side. This was at the same time an exercise in arrangement, and enabled the pupils later to quickly lay their hand on the motifs when they needed them. As I myself preferred drawing to cutting out, I inadvertently acquired a little training in the latter.

In Fig. 4-3, the following stitches were used:
A1. Half a tulip was drawn with whole cross-stitches.
A2. The tulip was unfolded, painted, and the colors specified with the aid of symbols.
B1. The half knapweed was drawn with indications for cross-stitches, and a few backstitches and shifted-over cross-stitches.
B2. After the knapweed was unfolded and painted, the colors were specified with the aid of symbols. A few backstitches in shade No. 216 lie on top of the cross-stitches, which are in shade No. 26.
C. The asymmetrical knapweed, drawn with whole cross-stitches and backstitches, was also painted.
D. Whole cross-stitches and ¾ cross-stitches are shown.
E. In this flower, only whole cross-stitches are needed.
F. More whole cross-stitches.
G. In this motif, whole cross-stitches, ¾ cross-stitches, and backstitches passing over 1 and 2 threads are used.
H. Whole cross-stitches again.
I. The tree motif is in whole cross-stitches.
J. Shown are whole cross-stitches, shifted-over cross-stitches, and ¾ cross-stitches. The flower is in blue, shade No. 228.

4-3. The paper cutouts from Fig. 4-2 have been drawn on graph paper for cross-stitching.

95

I drew one of the two trees in Fig. 4-4 for cross-stitching, but when it came to the embroidery (see Fig. 4-5), I made the tree a little taller and the ducks a little smaller. I used Danish Flower Thread in shades of green, brown, and blue on linen 10.5.

The other motif (see Fig. 4-6) was worked in stem stitches, satin stitches, and daisy stitches with white D.M.C. on white voile. (See pp. 126 and 131 for the stitching instructions.)

The embroideries that were made from the trees in Fig. 4-2 are shown in Figs. 4-7 and 4-8, and they display a different technique. (See Chapter 5.) The tree on the left is worked in stem stitches and satin stitches with red silk on Italian canvas, while the tree on the right is worked in French knots, coral stitches, and stem stitches, with Danish Flower Thread in shades of green, brown, and white on pale green linen.

The illustrations shown are a little smaller than life-size.

4-4

4-5

4-6

4-7

4-8

97

98

*Facing page, at left,* 4-9. Paper cutout of dandelions.

*Facing page, at right,* 4-10. Cross-stitch pattern for mini bellpull with dandelions.

4-11. Finished embroidery of mini bellpull with dandelions.

The information for the embroidery shown in Fig. 4-11 is:
Mini bellpull, dandelions, L.N. 3599.
Size: 2⅜" x 10¾".
Cutting measurements: 2 pieces, 5⅛" x 13½".
Thread: Danish Flower Thread in blue, shade No. 17.
Material: Linen II, bleached.
Technique: Cross-stitching and backstitching.

Measure a point 1½" in and 1½" down at the top left-hand corner of the material which corresponds to the top left-hand stitch of the border, in order to find the beginning point of the embroidery. The arrow on the drawing marks the center of the mini bellpull. At this point the same 3 flowers are repeated once more.

To mount the embroidery, fold 4 threads under on all four sides. The hanging bar and finial, which are 2½" wide, are attached and sewn down with small backstitches. Cut out the backing to correspond exactly with the front piece and sew it all the way around.

# Chapter 5.

# DESIGNS EMPLOYING OTHER EMBROIDERY STITCHES

During my 30 years of collaboration with the Handcraft Guild, I have been almost solely concerned with cross-stitch embroidery. The patterns I have created for predesigned embroideries constitute only a fraction of my output—not because I lack interest in this type of embroidery, but rather because cross-stitch designing has absorbed most of my time.

As models for the predesigned embroideries I use pressed flowers, my own watercolors, and drawings and motifs, just as with my cross-stitch designs; I often need a combination of them all, especially for patterns with many plants.

The procedure, however, is very different, as illustrated—though in only one detail of the complete drawing—in the following pages. Figures 5-1 through 5-4 depict the method for drawing the pattern and transferring it to the material:

First I prepare a pencil drawing of stems and flowers on tracing paper (Fig. 5-1); the drawing is the same size I have in mind for the finished embroidery.

Now I transfer the drawing to a piece of colored cardboard (5-2) by placing the cardboard on the bottom, with a sheet of blue carbon on top of it, and on top of the carbon paper, the tracing paper with the drawing. I fasten the 3 papers together firmly, then press through the outlines with a hard pencil, so that a sharp outline appears on the cardboard. Finally, I paint over the design with thick white paint, and then determine which stitches to employ. It is also possible to buy white carbon paper, but I use it only with dark cardboard.

I now draw the motif for pricking (5-3) by putting a piece of tracing paper on top of the cardboard. This time I trace the pattern seen through the paper with as few lines as possible. One line is sufficient for a stem, for instance. The leaf I wish to appliqué has to be drawn separately, and slightly bigger, because the edges have to be folded under and seamed. The ribs need only to be drawn on this leaf. (For appliqué instructions, see p. 131.)

Now the drawing has to be pricked, i.e., all the lines have to be perforated, and for that we have an electric pricking machine. This operation must be carried out by a practiced hand, since it is of the utmost importance that the contours not be distorted.

Finally the drawing can be transferred to the material (5-4). A dye is pressed through all the holes in the drawing by means of a piece of rolled-up felt called a "major." The drawing must not be allowed to slip during this step, so heavy weights—not thumbtacks—are placed on it. The weights must be so positioned that it is possible to raise the drawing at the bottom in order to see that the operation is being carried out properly.

If it is not possible to use the methods mentioned above, we can recommend a good but more primitive method that is clearly illustrated in *Crewel Embroidery*, a book by Erica Wilson.

5-1

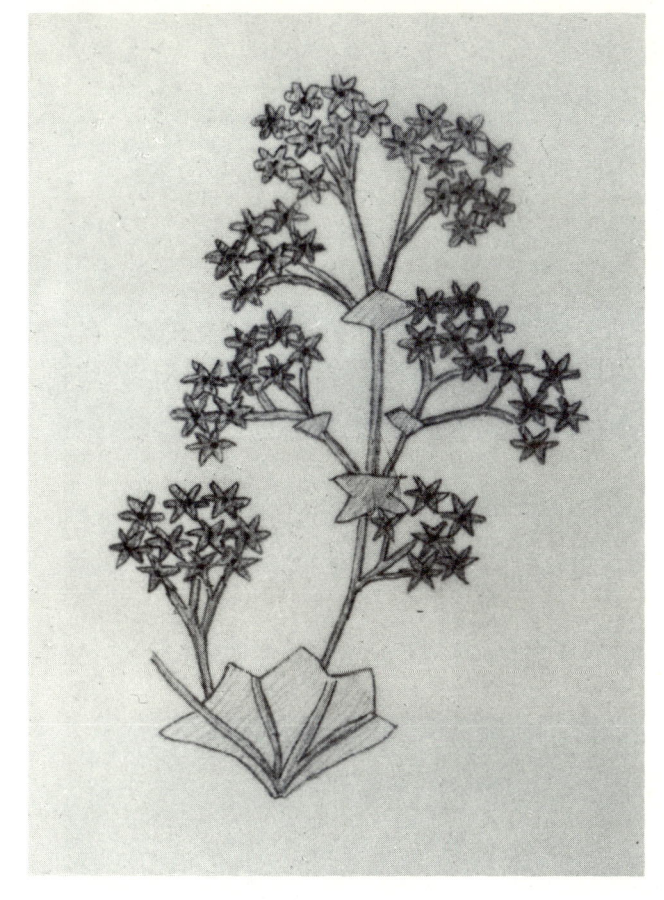

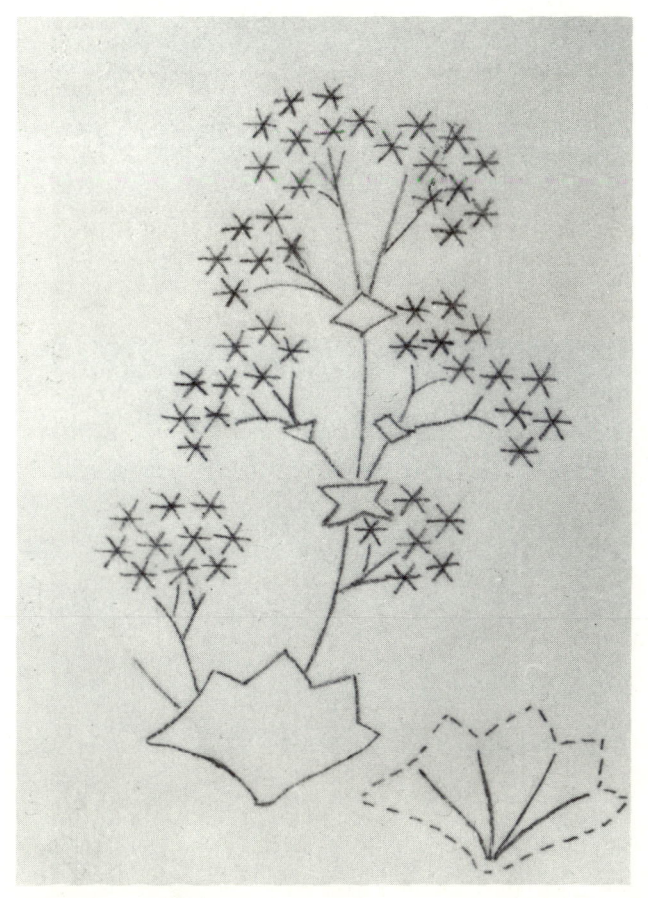

5-2

5-3

5-4

101

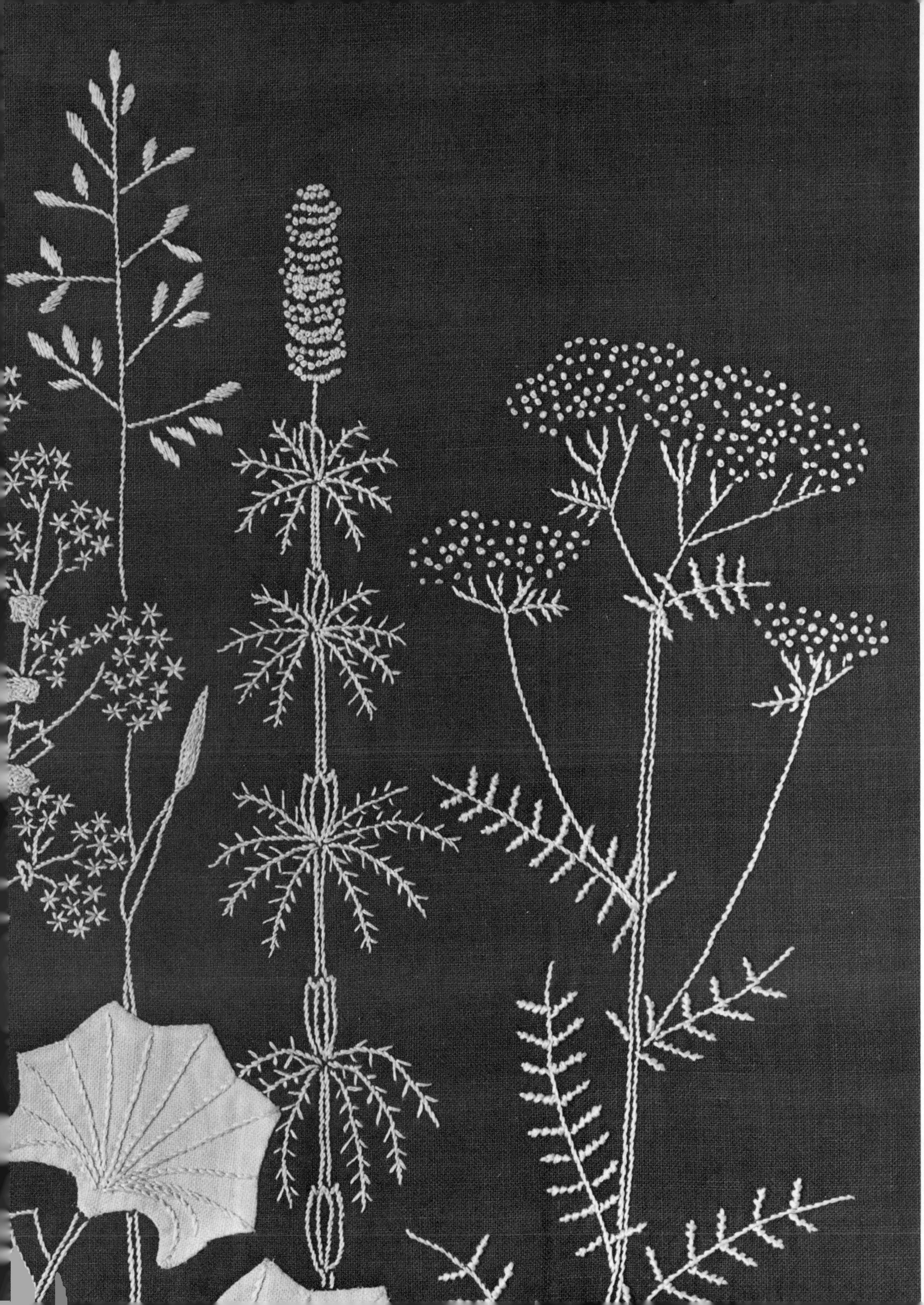

5-6. Lady's-mantle cushion, L.N. 1883.
Size: 18¾" x 21⅝".
Thread: Clark white.
Material: cotton.
Appliqué material: Irish linen.
Technique: stem stitch, coral stitch, satin stitch, French knots, long-armed cross-stitch, and long stitches worked from the outside in toward the middle; and the appliqué technique. (For coral stitch instructions, see p. 126, and French knot instructions, p. 129.)

*Facing page,* 5-5. A close to life-size detail of lady's-mantle cushion shown in Fig. 5-6.

103

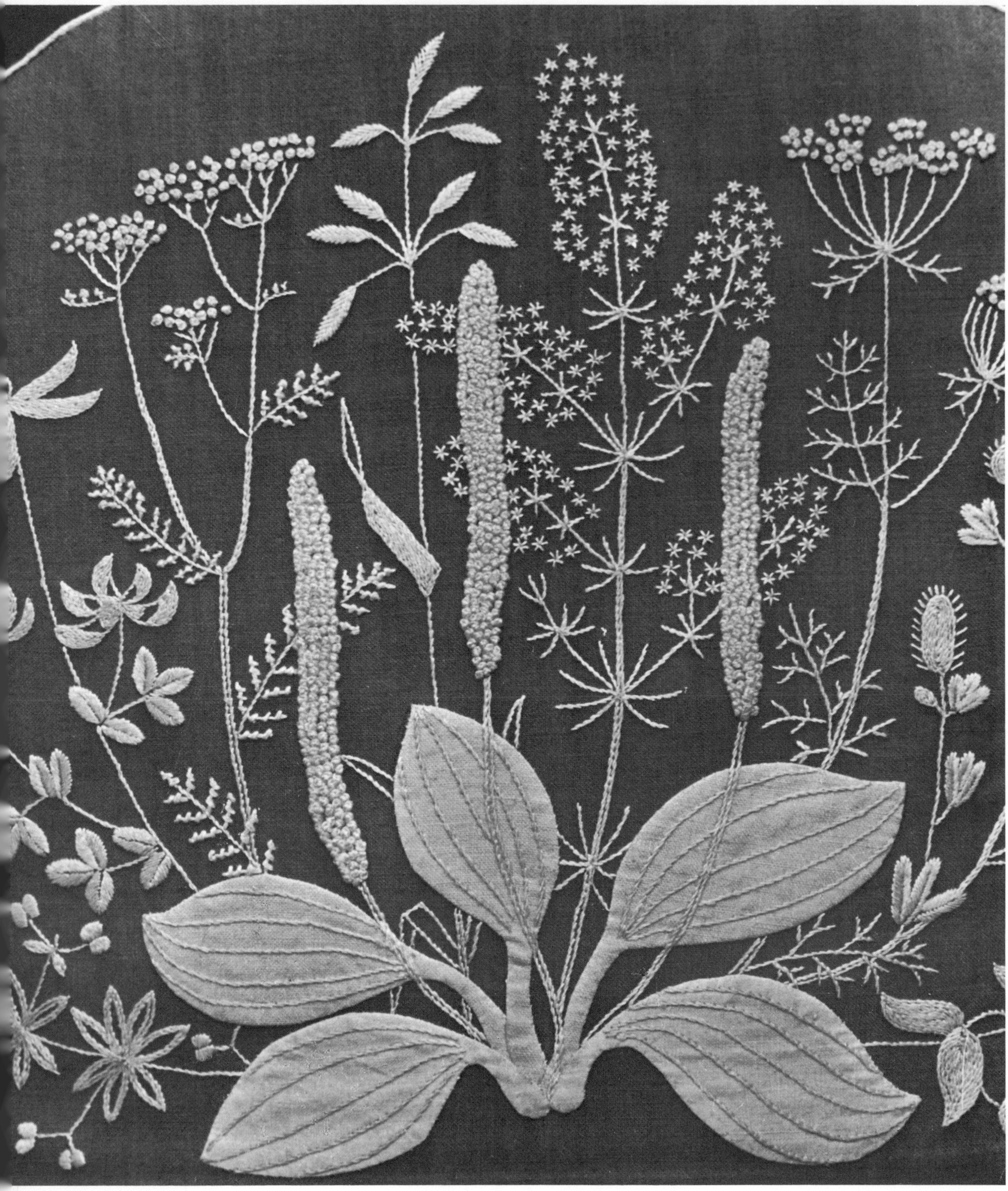

After having drawn the design for the lady's-mantle cushion illustrated in Fig. 5-6, I continued in the same fashion. In each case I chose the embroidery technique that best suited the plant. For both embroideries (Figs. 5-6 and 5-8), I found it best to use a plant in appliqué as a central, heavier motif. My models consisted of various florae and my pressed flowers. Since the embroideries are worked in white only, the cushion and tea cozy can be sewn on blue, green, or red cotton material.

*Facing page:* 5-7. A life-size detail of the tea cozy with plantains shown in full in Fig. 5-8.

5-8. Tea cozy with plantain, L.N. 1904.
Size: 11⅜″ x 14⅛″.
Material: cotton.
Appliqué material: Irish linen.
Technique: stem stitch, coral stitch, satin stitch, French knots, long-armed cross-stitch, and long stitches worked from the outside in toward the middle; and the appliqué technique. (Instructions for sewing the long-armed cross-stitch and long stitches are on p. 129.).

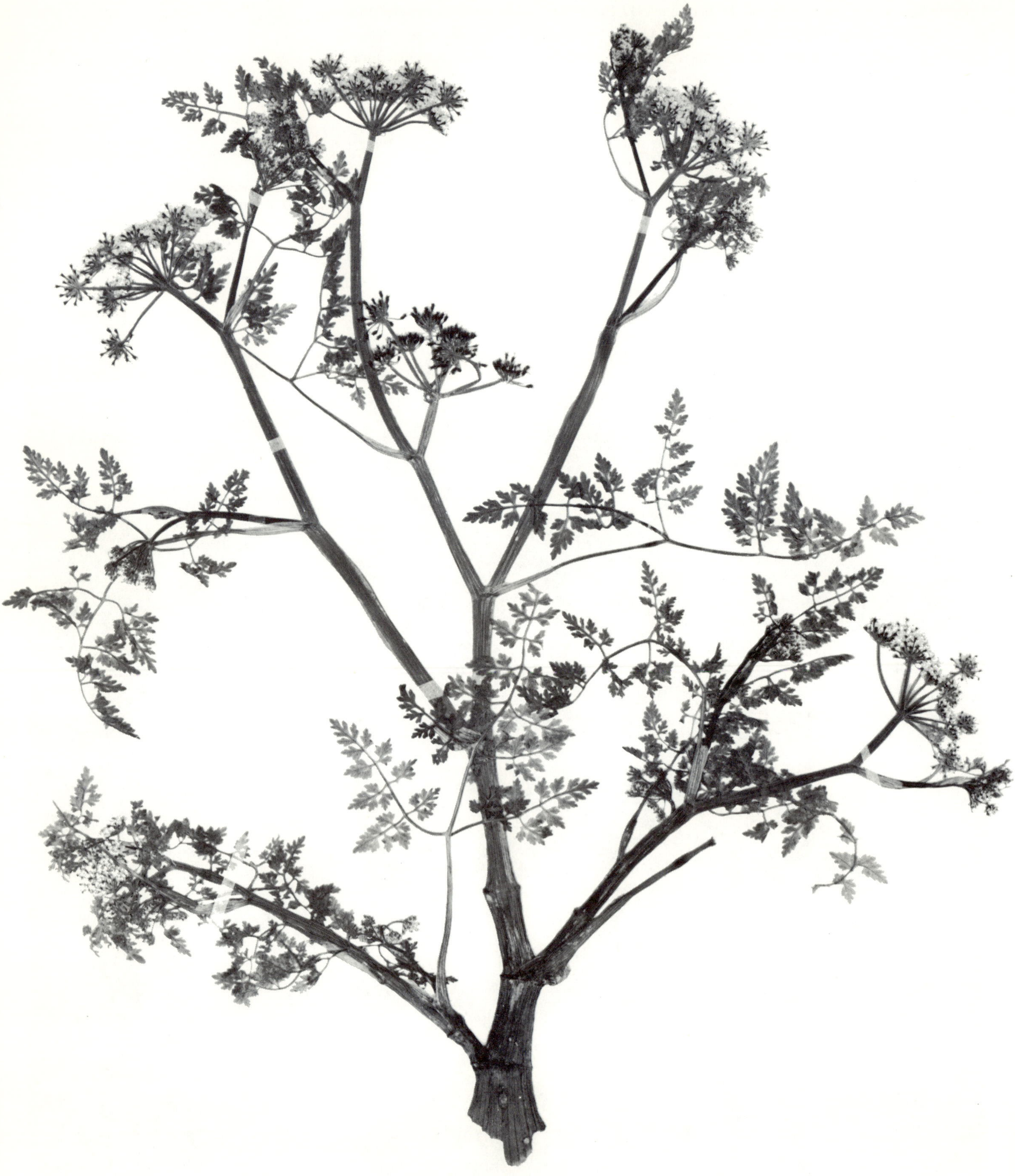

5-10. A less than life-size working drawing for a cushion with the water fennel motif.

*Facing page:* 5-9. The pressed plant, water fennel, known in the herbarium as Louis Fog. For the color drawing of this plant, see pp. 110-111.

*Facing page:* 5-13. Pencil drawing of a wild carrot that has stopped flowering.

5-11. Cushion with water fennel, L.N. 3181.
Size: 19½" x 19½".
Thread: flax and Danish Flower Thread.
Colors: Pale yellow-green No. 592; medium green No. 519; and white No. 0.
Material: navy-blue linen.
Technique: stem stitch, daisy stitch, and French knots.
By studying the drawing on p. 107, you can bring this pattern up to life-size.

5-12. Life-size embroidery detail from the cushion with water fennel.

In preparation for the cushion cover with the wild carrot motif (p. 112), I picked the top of a wild carrot plant that had stopped flowering. The drawing shown in Fig. 5-13 is not a true copy of the plant, for while drawing I simplified it greatly. There were really many more seed capsules in the background, but I only drew what I could think of using. Shortly afterwards I started on the pattern itself. As one can see, I more or less retained the number and shape of the capsules, but spread out the motif so that it filled the shape of the cushion better.

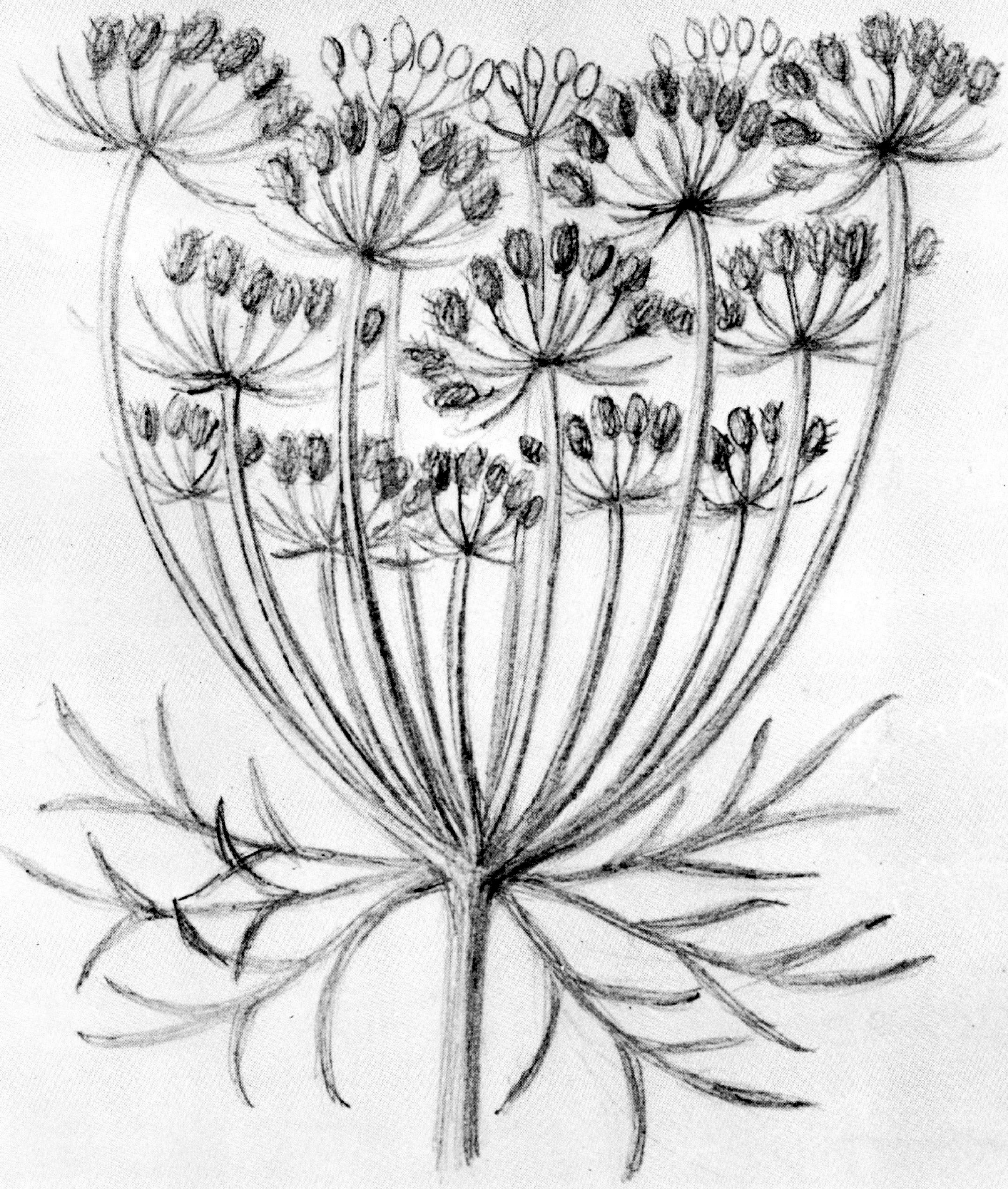

A detail of the water fennel drawing.

Color drawing of the water fennel plant discussed on pp. 106-108.

5-14. Cushion cover with wild carrot motif, L.N. 2138.
Size: 14⅛" x 15⅛".
Cutting measurements: 31¼" x 17½".
Thread: flax.
Material: German linen.
Technique: stem stitches and long stitches.

5-15. Detail from Fig. 5-14.

I used only three colors in the cushion: medium green, pale yellow-green, and golden gray.

The leaves are in medium green, the stems and the three small umbels are in pale yellow-green, while the large umbels are in golden gray. The cushion has a green piping.

# EXERCISE: CREATING A LARGER-SCALE DRAWING

A pattern which is too small, and which one would like to draw for pricking, can be enlarged—as with Fig. 5-16—by dividing the motif up into squares. The same number of squares is then drawn larger until the motif is of the right size. Even if you are inexperienced, you can draw the motif in this way, provided you make sure that all lines fall the same way and within the same squares as in the smaller drawing.

5-16. The wild carrot pattern in smaller than life-size scale.

5-17. Drawing exercise continued: a life-size detail.

It is possible to continue, as illustrated in Fig. 5-17, until all the 36 squares are brought up to life-size. I have already put in the beginning of the drawing; so it is just a matter of adding the rest of the lines in the correct squares.

Use pencil and tracing paper. In the last drawing, the line must be clear and accurate.

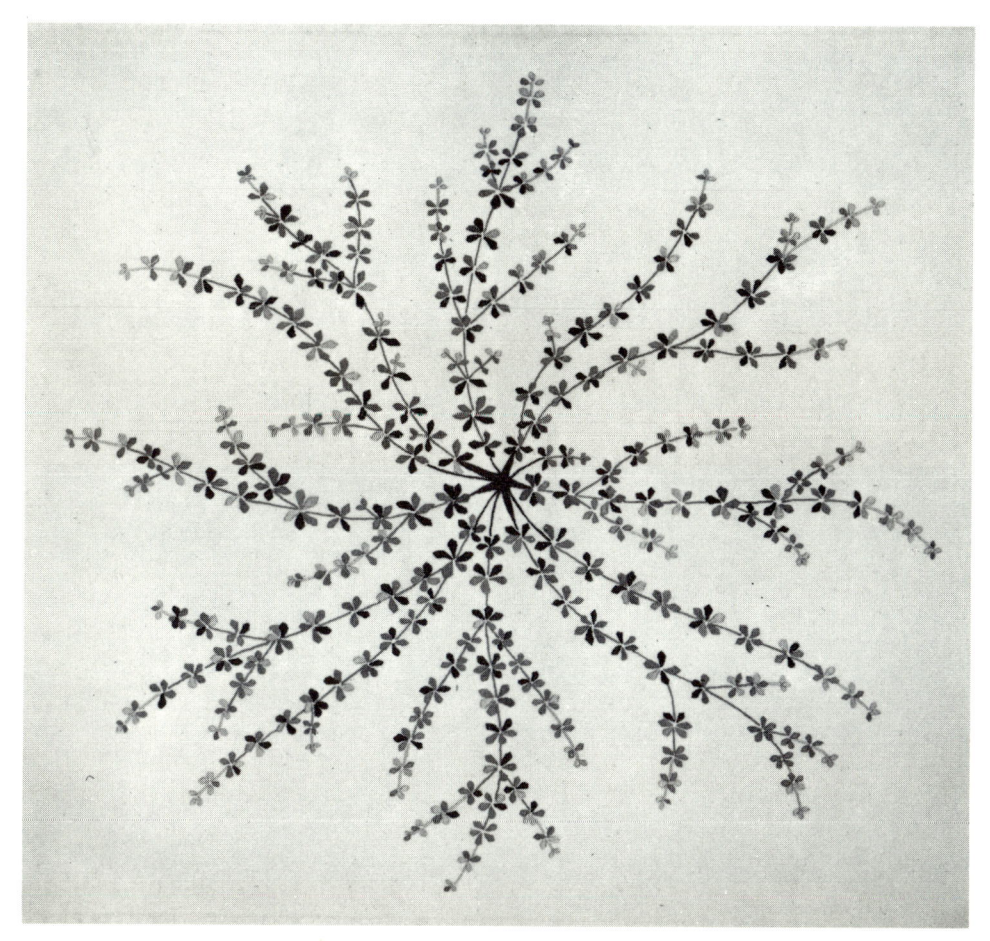

5-18. Cushion with bedstraw motif, L.N. 1958.
Size: 16⅜" x 15½".
Thread: Danish Flower Thread.
Material: Irish linen.
Technique: satin stitch and stem stitch.

Some years ago, one day when I was out with the Danish Botanical Society, I found a heath bedstraw, which was spread out somewhat in the fashion illustrated on the cushion above. I picked a couple of stems and painted from them with watercolors when I got home (see Fig. 5-19). The only thing I could do while in the forest was to make a careful study of the way in which the plant grew, for it appealed to me and I thought of doing something with it.

5-19. Painting of the heath bedstraw which became the motif for the cushion in Fig. 5-18.

5-20. I took one of the stems from the bedstraw cushion and drew it for pricking. The drawing is shown life-size.

5-21. The embroidery was done in satin stitches and stem stitches.

5-22. Table mat with bay willow, corner motif, L.N. 1929.
Size: 11⅝" x 16⅝".
Cutting measurements: 13¼" x 18".
Thread: Clark, white.
Material: green cotton No. 14.
Appliqué material: Irish linen.
Technique: Stem stitch, French knots, cross-stitch, and appliqué.

The bay willow motif was drawn from various florae, first for a cross-stitch design for one of my books, and then for an appliqué, as shown above, in which some other kinds of embroidery stitches were also employed.

The drawing for pricking is to be seen life-size in Fig. 5-23. Every appliqué leaf is given a number, which is transferred to the green material. The leaves that are to be appliquéd are drawn slightly bigger. They are transferred onto white linen by means of a light pricking, and the appropriate numbers are added.

For both drawings, use pencil on tracing paper. Two lines running along the table mat border mark the place for two rows of stem stitches. These are followed by a row of French knots that go, as closely as the eye can judge, in a line exactly in the middle of the 2 rows. The material is folded under for the hem about ⅛" outside the outermost row of stem stitches and it is hemmed in the usual way along the innermost row, using an ordinary hemstitch.

5-23. Life-size drawing of bay willow motif for pricking.

5-24. Appliqué leaves drawn life-size for pricking.

119

# Chapter 6.
# STITCHERY TECHNIQUES AND MATERIALS

### Linens

Every time I begin a new cross-stitch pattern I decide immediately which of the 8 linens my pattern is to be sewn on. Not only must the number of stitches to be used be counted out on the material and marked out on the paper, but it is also very important that the pattern and material harmonize. For a plant with broad lines linen D is suitable, but for delicate plants composed of small characteristic shapes I would naturally choose one of the finer linens.

Usually, a pattern looks best on the original linen, but as I have now and again transferred my pattern to another linen and obtained good results, you might say that these are the exceptions that prove the rule.

However, some patterns cannot stand being transferred to a different type of linen, and other patterns cannot be worked on a finer—or coarser—type of linen, because of color considerations. My cow parsnip, for instance, cannot be worked on a finer linen requiring the use of a single thread, for in certain places I have had to use two different colors at once, in order to produce a mottled effect that cannot be gotten with only a single thread.

On the finest linens I sew with a single thread of Danish Flower Thread, or with two threads of Clark or D.M.C. With coarser linens there is more choice: on D linen, either 2 or 3 threads of Danish Flower Thread may be used, or 4 strands of Clark or D.M.C. On linen Hanne, either 3 threads of Danish Flower Thread or 6 threads of Clark or D.M.C. are used.

The linens are reproduced life-size in Fig. 6-1. The linen Hanne is handwoven, while all the others are machine-woven. Even-weave natural linen can be substituted for the specific ones I use if you remember that linen Hanne has 7 threads to the inch; linen D, 10 threads; linen 10.5, 14 threads; linen II, 16 threads; and linen I, 18 threads. I use canvas needles without points, and I have suggested needle types under the different linens. However, if you cannot obtain the particular needle number I mention, it does not make that much difference if you use the next closest number available to you.

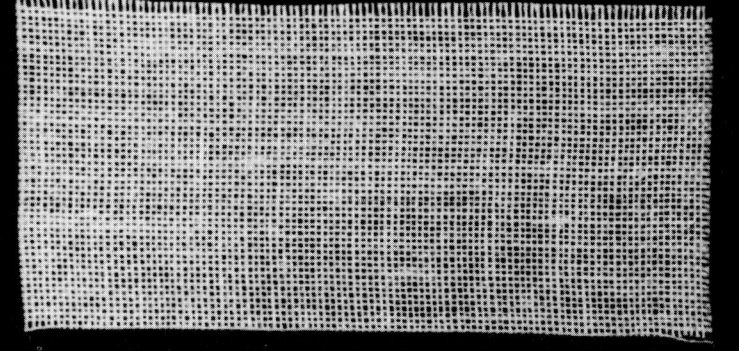

Linen II, unbleached.
Needle No. 25.

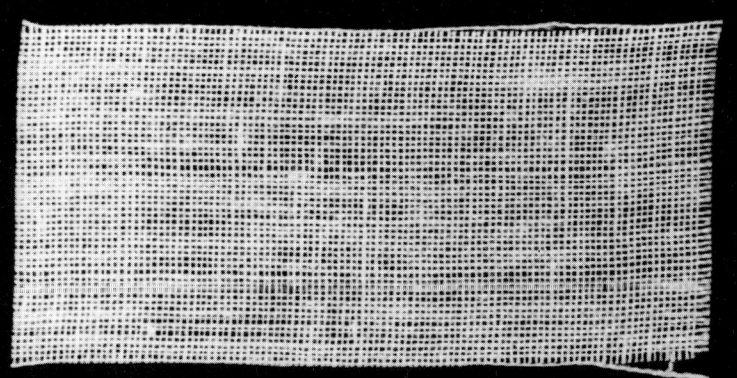

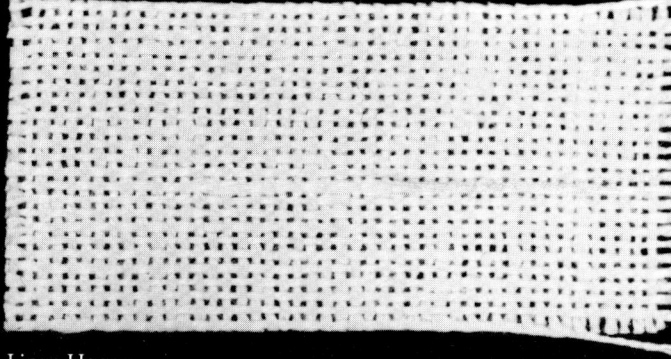

Linen Hanne.
Needle No. 20.

Linen II, bleached.
Needle No. 25.

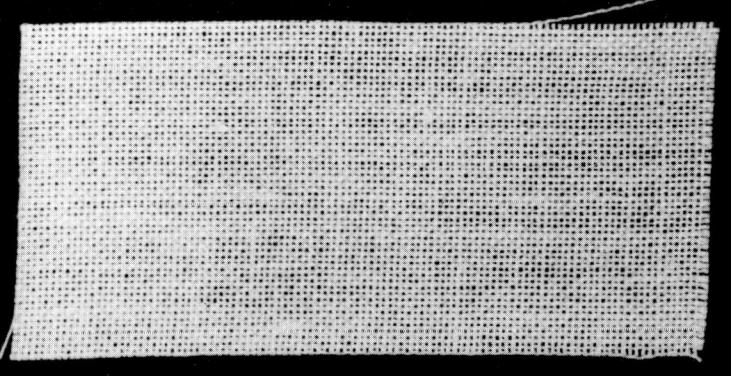

Linen D, unbleached.
Needle No. 21.

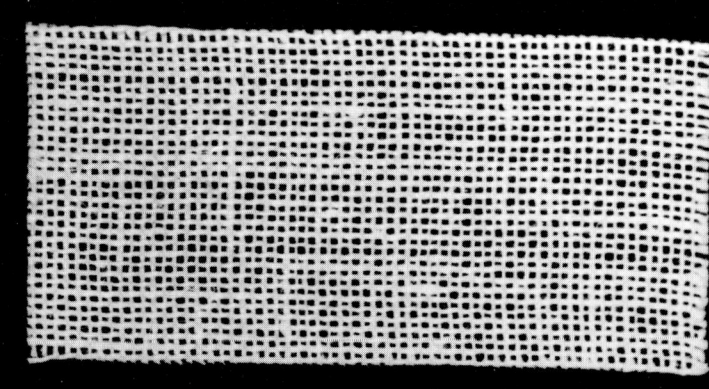

Linen IA.
Needle No. 24.

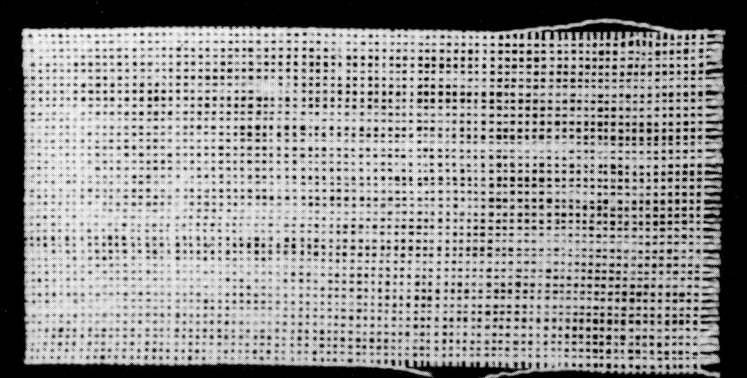

Linen D, bleached.
Needle No. 21.

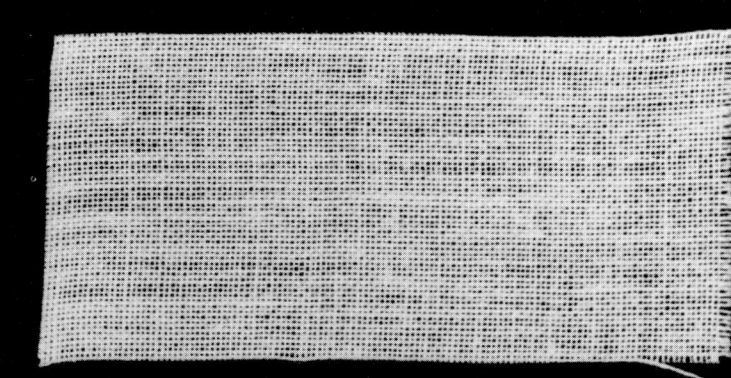

Linen 10.5.
Needle No. 24.

Linen I.
Needle No. 25.

6-1. The 8 different linens for cross-stitch.

*Overleaf:* The Danish Flower Threads, less than life-size.

121

DANISH FLOWER THREAD NUMBERS

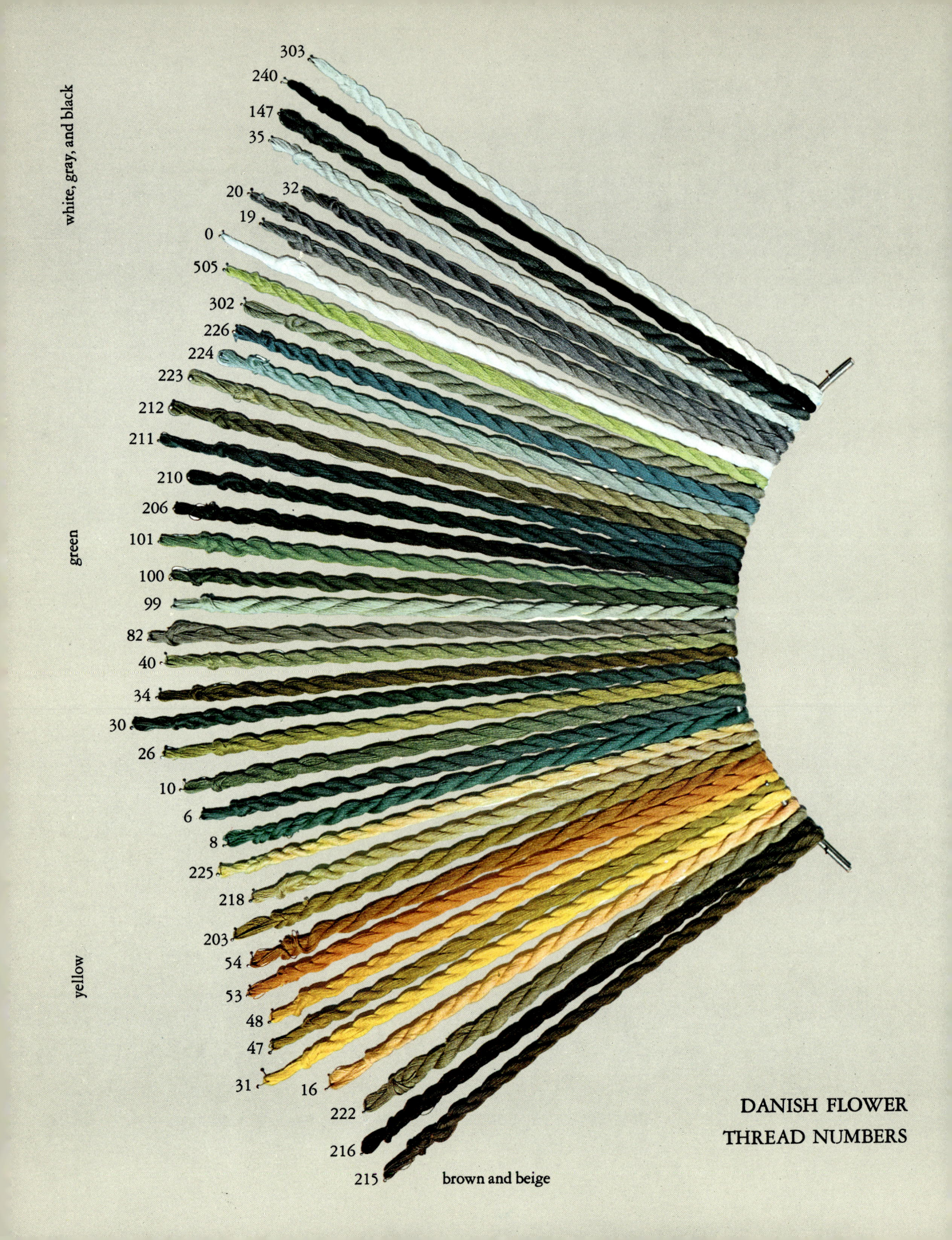

See page 135 for information as to where the shade card and skeins of Danish Flower Thread may be obtained.

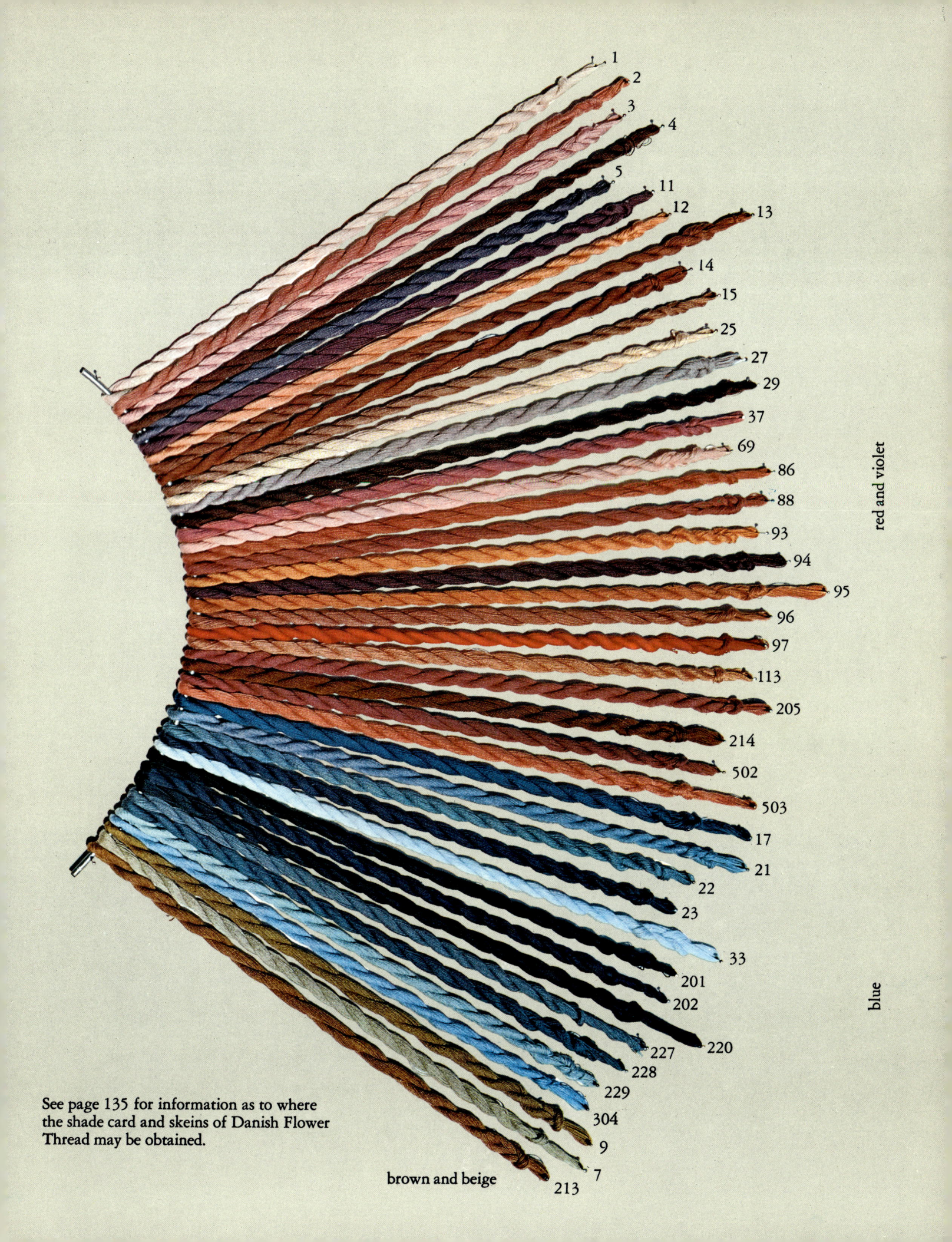

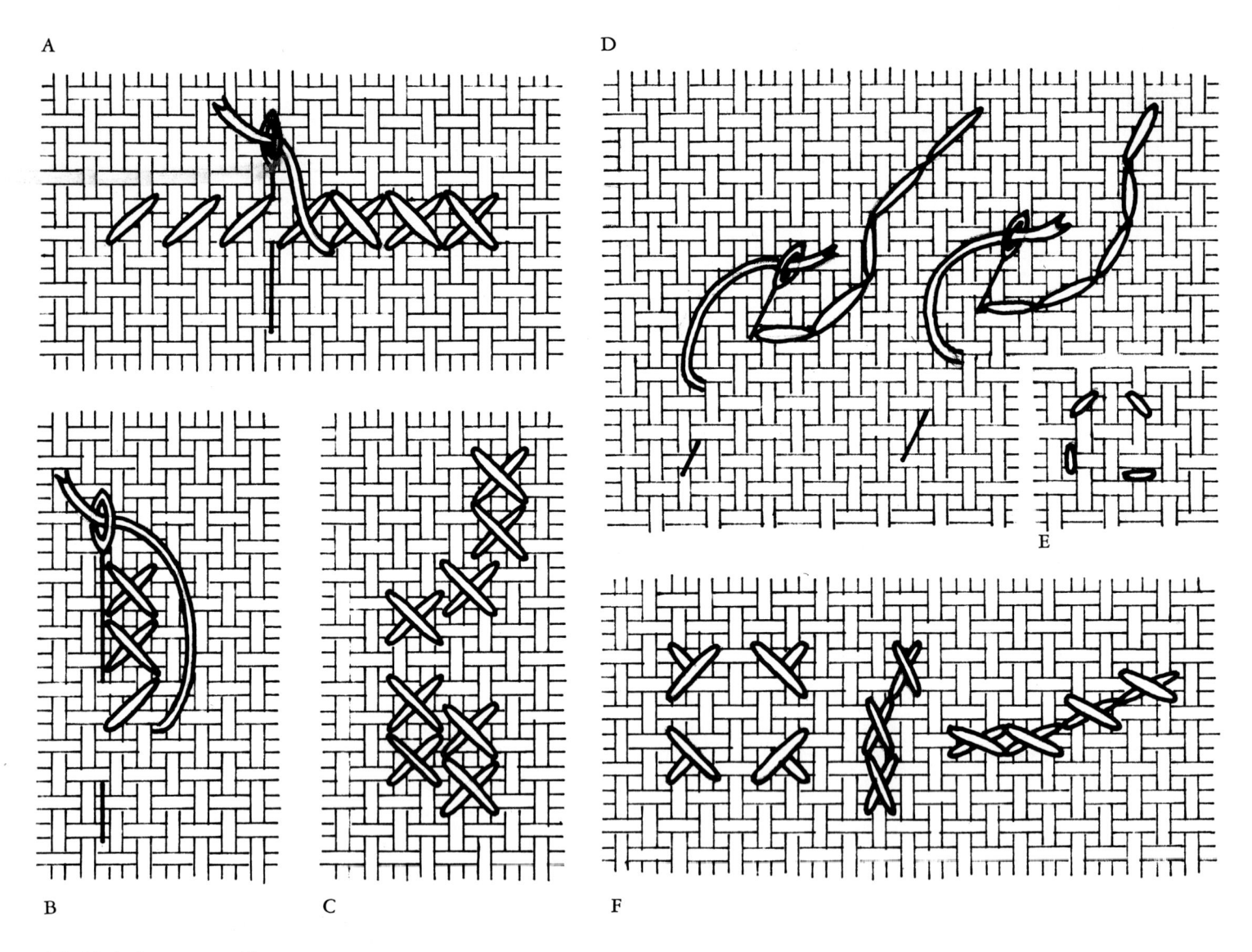

6-2. Stitch diagrams, topside.

## STITCHERY TECHNIQUES

In Fig. 6-2, note:

A. In a row of cross-stitches worked from left to right, all the under stitches are worked first, passing diagonally over 2 threads, from the bottom left-hand corner to the top right-hand corner. To complete the cross-stitches, the covering stitches are worked on the way back, from right to left.

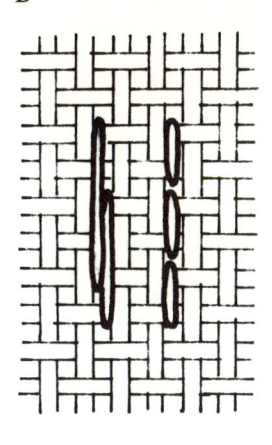

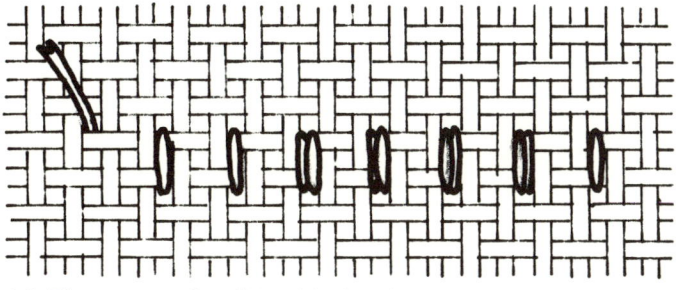

6-3. The reverse sides of Fig. 6-2 (A and B) show vertical stitches only.

B. With cross-stitches worked from above downwards, each stitch is done completely—under and over—so that the covering stitch follows the same direction as in the drawing.

The reverse side of A and B must only show vertical stitches (see Fig. 6-3).

C. Cross-stitches shifted over in relation to each other.

D. In two different rows of stem stitches, on the left, the two top stitches run 2 threads sideways and 2 threads down, one stitch runs 2 threads vertically and another stitch runs 2 threads horizontally. On the right, the top stitch runs 2 threads down, but only 1 thread sideways, and the fourth stitch runs 2 threads sideways and 1 thread down. In addition, there is one vertical stitch and one horizontal stitch.

E. Four stem stitches, passing over either a single thread or a single intersection.

F. On the left are four ¾ cross-stitches. On the right, half cross-stitches pass over 1 thread in one direction and 2 threads in the other direction.

125

6-4  A

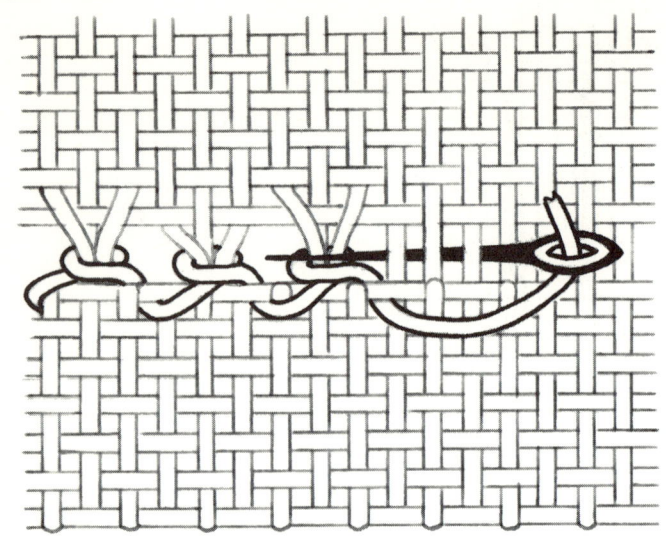

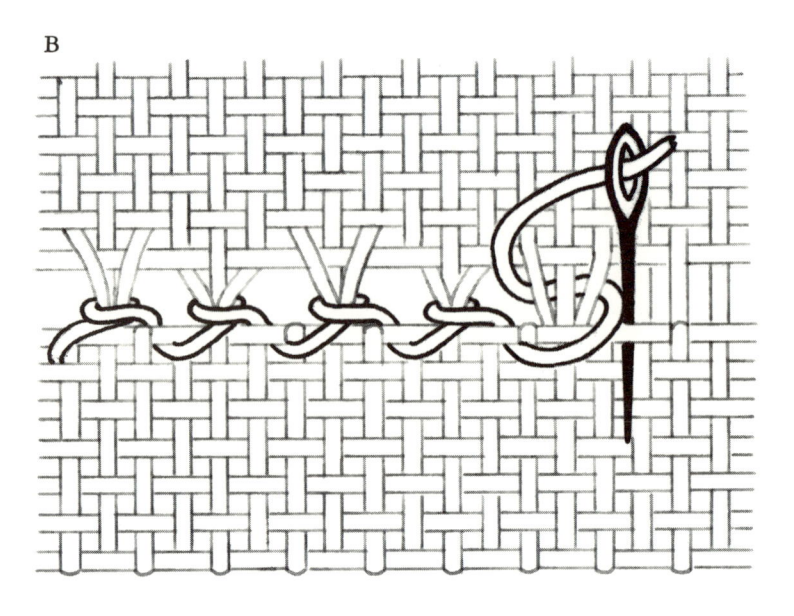

B

In 1930, when I first started to draw plant motifs for cross-stitching, I used a very simple technique. It had its own charm, but the drawback was that many of my patterns produced in this way were botanically incorrect. By developing a new technique, however, which employed not only whole cross-stitches but stem stitches, cross-stitches shifted over by a thread, and half cross-stitches when necessary, they came to resemble the plants more. For big plants with simple shapes, however, or when working on canvas, I still just use the whole cross-stitch by itself.

The *hem stitch* is a particular kind of stitch needed for hemming, with or without the use of drawn threads. Naturally, it is worked on the reverse side of the pattern. (See Fig. 6-4.) In "A," the needle passes under a group of threads from right to left. Then, in "B," one small stitch is made down into the hem just to the right of the threads previously encircled. Whenever the hem stitch has been employed in the various embroideries in this book, the threads have not been drawn.

6-5

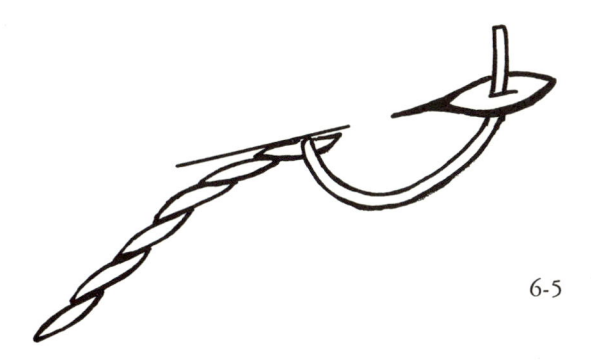

The *stem stitch* (Fig. 6-5) is worked along a line, passing from left to right. The needle emerges at the beginning of the line, and while the thread is held firmly under the thumb of the left hand, it pierces the material a little to the right, emerging a short distance to the left. The thread is pulled taut and another stitch is made, this time the needle emerging at the point where the previous stitch ended.

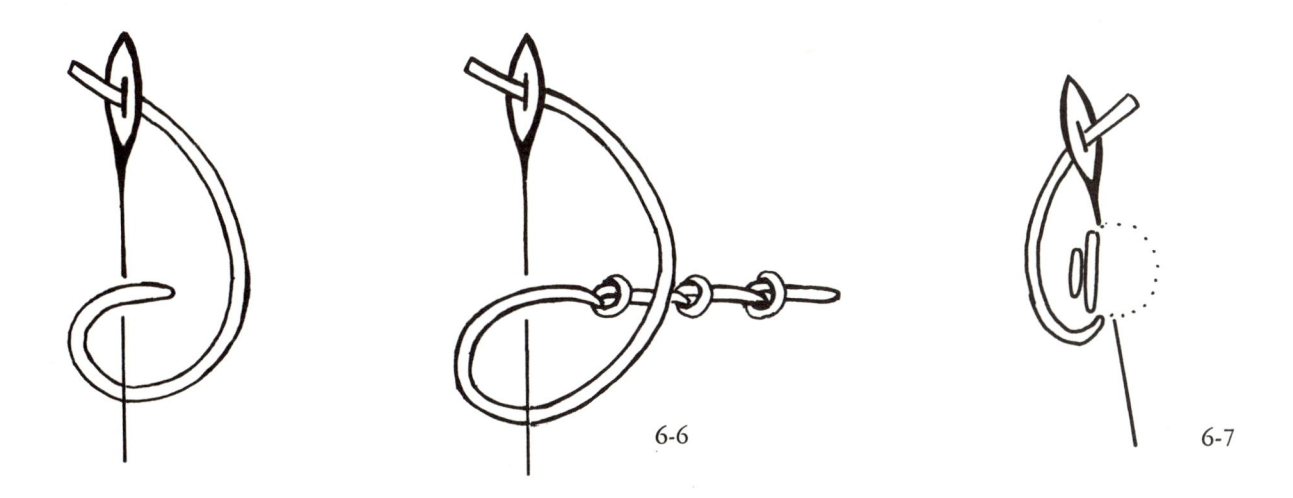

6-6  6-7

The *coral stitch* (6-6) is also worked along a line, passing from right to left. The needle emerges at the beginning of the line. The thread is laid along the line and held firmly with the left hand. The needle then pierces the material a little above the line and emerges a little below it, so that the needle is at right angles to the line. The needle is pulled through, thus forming a small knot.

The *satin stitch* (6-7) is worked in such a way that the space to be sewn is completely covered and the threads lie so close together that no material is visible. The length of the stitches depends on the shape to be filled in.

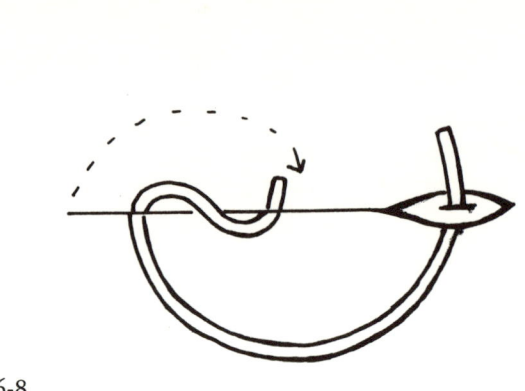

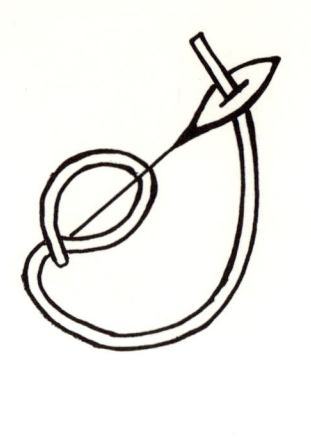

6-8

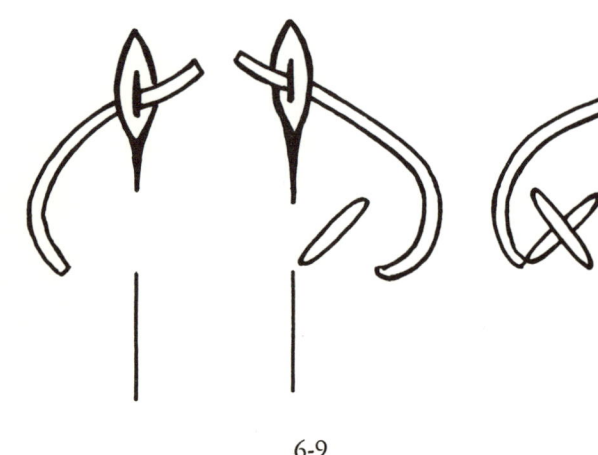

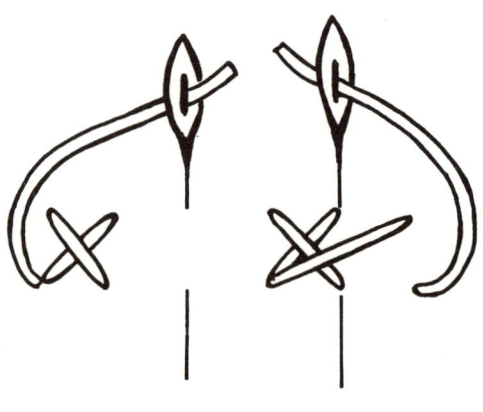

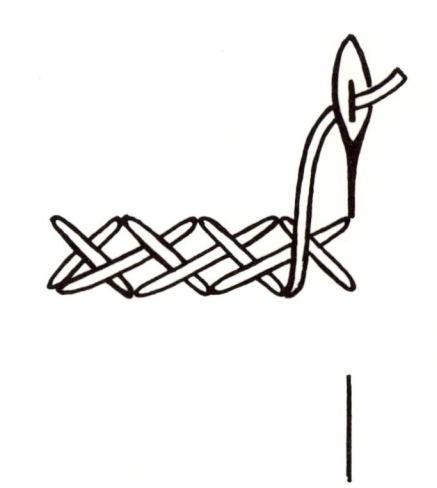

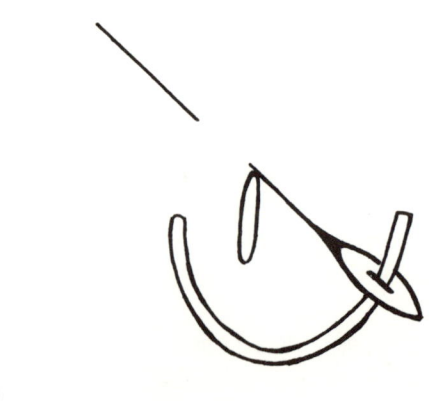

6-9

6-10

With *French knots* (6-8) the needle emerges from the material at the spot where the knot is to be, and the thread is held down firmly with the left thumb. The needle is then twisted round the thread two or three times and then the point of the needle is turned round completely, as shown by the arrow, and inserted close to where the thread first emerged. While the needle is still sticking halfway through the material, and while still holding the thread firmly with the left thumb as near the knot as possible, the twists of thread are tightened carefully around the needle. The needle is then drawn through. Each knot should be completed before starting on the next one.

The *long-armed cross-stitch* (6-9) is a kind of cross-stitch which is worked in horizontal rows, first from left to right and then from right to left; two consecutive rows must never be worked in the same direction. The material is pierced from below and an ordinary cross-stitch, i.e., one passing over 2 threads in each direction, is completed. Afterwards, another stitch is worked, and this time the stitch from below passes 4 threads across and 2 threads in height, whereas the stitch from above consists of the usual 2 threads in height and 2 threads in width. The stitch is continued in this fashion, by working a long stitch from below and a short stitch from above until the row is completed. As can be seen from the drawing, the row ends with a short stitch from below, so in order to proceed to the next row, it is necessary to make an extra stitch which ends right down in the row below. This row is worked from right to left, again beginning with an ordinary cross-stitch followed by a long stitch passing from right to left and a short stitch passing from left to right.

*Long stitches* (6-10), which can be used for working small stars, pass from the outside in toward the middle.

6-11

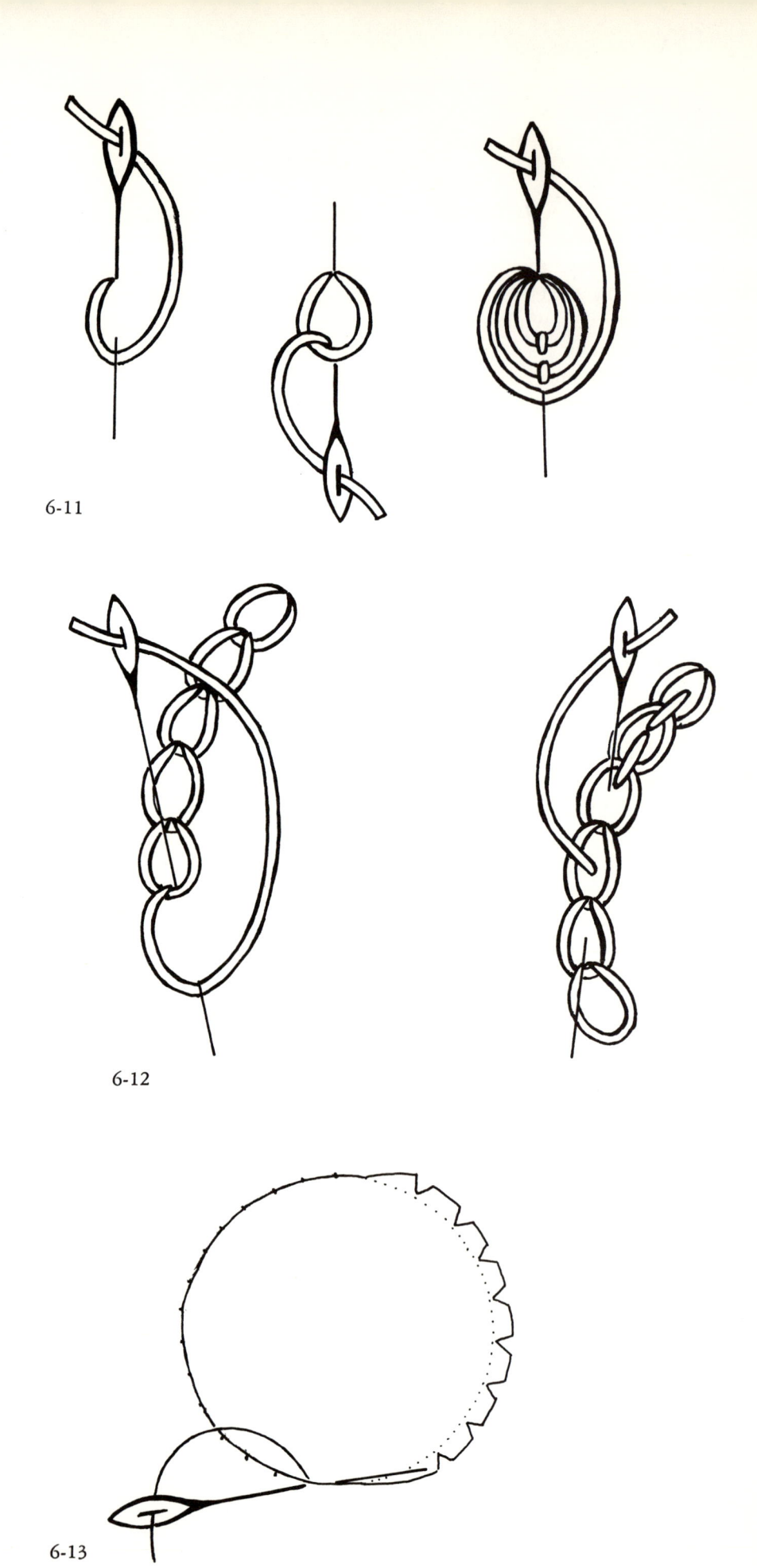

6-12

6-13

The *daisy stitch* (6-11) is a simple chain stitch, worked from above and downward toward the embroiderer. The needle emerges at the required spot and the thread is held down a little to the left with the left thumb. The needle is inserted again at the exact spot where it came out to emerge a little farther below, the needle passing over the thread. It is then drawn through, thus forming a little loop, and pierces the material again on the other side of this loop. If further daisy stitches are required, a slightly bigger stitch may be made to encircle the first one, and so on.

To get *backstitched chain stitches* (6-12), first a row of chain stitches is worked. The needle pierces the material, and the thread is placed on the left-hand side and held down firmly with the left hand. The needle is then inserted into the exact spot where the thread first emerged and is brought out again a short distance below so that it lies over the loose thread. The needle is pulled through, thus forming a loop. The process is repeated until all the chain stitches are worked. Then the chain is backstitched. The needle emerges in the middle of the second chain stitch, and pierces the material again in the middle of the first chain stitch, to emerge again in the middle of the third. The process is repeated, always stitching back into the middle of the chain stitch directly above.

For *appliqué* (6-13), the material to be appliquéd to the background material is cut out approximately $1/5''$ on the outside of the outlined shape. Small wedges are cut out in order to simplify the folding under of the edge and to prevent its being too bulky. The appliqué is then stitched very carefully onto the ground material, with tiny invisible hem stitches, working always from right to left and folding in the seam bit by bit with the needle.

132

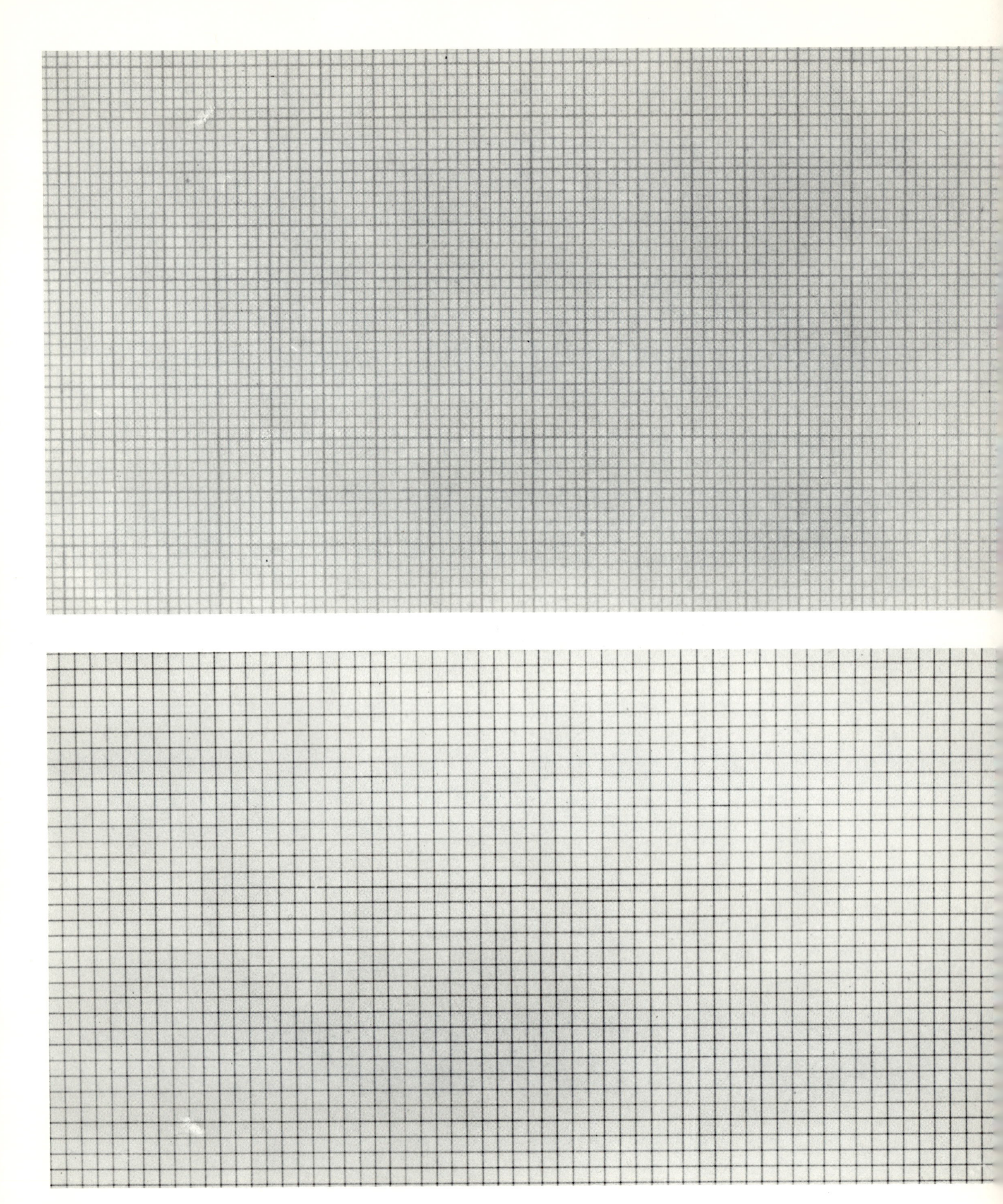

# GRAPH PAPER

There are many kinds of graph paper available in stores. The paper, which may have big or small squares, may either be left blank, or again subdivided into 5 or 10 smaller squares. Finally, the lines may be in different colors, including red, gray, or black. Graph paper with small squares is the best choice when drawing patterns for fine materials, whereas paper with big squares is preferable when using coarser materials. For the finer linens in the book, 2 mm. paper, to be seen in Fig. 6-14, can be recommended; for linen D, 3 mm. paper, shown in Fig. 6-15, is the most suitable. In some countries, instead of the metric system, graph paper is measured in terms of squares per inch. As a result, the size of the squares of American graph paper will differ from that of the squares in the graph paper illustrated in this book. (It is particularly difficult, I believe, to obtain large sheets of graph paper with squares as small as the 2mm. ones.) However, when you want to mark out the size of your embroidery, if you begin by counting the threads on the linen, as I have advised, and after that, count the same number of stitches down on the graph paper, the outcome will be satisfactory.

I draw on the graph paper with a soft pencil (such as 2B) and paint with a sable-hair paintbrush, No. 4, for small areas, and No. 5 or 6 for larger areas. A good stock of watercolor paints is necessary in order to get good results.

# TRACING PAPER

Ordinary tracing paper is readily available in most places. As mentioned before, the paper must be on the firm side to withstand all the erasing, but it is most important that the graph paper be clearly visible when the tracing paper is laid on top of it.

# WASHING AND IRONING INSTRUCTIONS

The Handcraft Guild's cotton weaving thread (Danish Flower Thread; see pp. 122-123) is dyed with the best and truest dyes that can be manufactured. The colored threads, however, often contain an excess of dye, which disappears in washing. It is important, therefore, that those who use the Danish Flower Thread follow exactly the instructions for washing and ironing given below.

WASHING. The embroidery must be rinsed several times in cold water, thereafter washed by hand in cold or lukewarm water with soap *flakes* (not powder), rinsed again in cold water several times, and then squeezed carefully and laid to dry between 2 white cloths.

IRONING. Never sprinkle the embroidery with water or roll it up; it must be laid with the right side down on a soft under-cloth. Place a piece of wrung-out gauze or some other thin material on top of it and iron until the material is dry. Then iron directly on the reverse side of the embroidery until it is quite dry.

*Facing page, top,* 6-14. 2 mm. graph paper showing the actual size of the squares. 15½" x 22" per sheet, I.C.P. 402.

*Facing page, bottom,* 6-15. 3 mm. graph paper showing the actual size of the squares. 14½" x 18" per sheet.
If desired, this paper can be obtained from the Danish Handcraft Guild (see p. 134 for the address).

The Danish Handcraft Guild
38 Vimmelskaftet
1161 Copenhagen K.
Denmark

All information concerning the patterns shown in this book, as well as orders for various articles such as those listed below, can be obtained on application to the Danish Handcraft Guild.

The patterns have been given a name and number, which should be quoted when ordering.

The following items can be ordered:

1. Finished embroideries.
2. Kits consisting of material, thread, cross-stitch pattern, and predesigned embroideries.
3. Linens by the yard.
4. A shade card for Danish Flower Thread.
5. Danish Flower Thread in skeins.
6. 3 mm. graph paper in sheets (big squares).
7. A catalogue of the Handcraft Guild's pattern books.
8. A catalogue illustrating the Handcraft Guild's embroideries in color.

All goods are sold only for private use and must not be ordered with the purpose of resale.

From I. C. Petersen's Stationers, Kirkestraede 1, 1073 Copenhagen K., Denmark, you can obtain 2 mm. graph paper (small squares) by the sheet, and also if you wish the tracing paper I use (111¼E smooth 0.90m. + 0.50m.).

Danish Flower Thread is available in the United States from:
The Artisans Guild, Inc., 10 B Street, Burlington, Mass. 01803

## PICTURE CREDITS

All the photographs were taken by Mathias except for the illustration of the Danish Flower Threads and Fig. 6-1; Fig. 1-31, which was taken by Bent Hassing; Fig. 1-39, which was taken by Elswing; and the pictures on pp. 107, 108, and 110-111, which were taken by Rotex.

# INDEX

Page numbers in italics indicate illustrations.

African marigold doily, 48
    pattern, *49*
Andersen, Hans Christian
    paper cutouts, 92
Appliqué technique, 100, *130*, 131

Backstitch
    design for, 66
Backstitched chain stitch, *130*, 131
Bay willow table mat, 117
    pattern, *119*
Bengtsson, Gerda
    development of work, 7-8
Black currant
    bellpull, 11
Black mullein wall hanging, 20
Boys' choir wall hanging, 59

Children's bellpull, 88
    pattern, *88*
Color
    of Danish Flower Threads, *122-123*
    and perspective, 90
    symbols for, *90*
Composition
    free, 10, *11*
    repeat, 10, *11, 32*
Coral stitch, *127*
Cow parsnip tapestry, 27
    linen for, 120
Cross-stitch, *124, 125, 128, 129*
    design for, 66
Cushion for Father, 58
Cushion for Mother, 60

Daisy stitch, *130*, 131
Dandelion cushion, 99
    pattern, *98*
Danish Flower Threads, 8, 29, 37, *122-123*
    washing and ironing instructions, 133
Danish Handcraft Guild, 6, 7, 8, 134
Danish samplers,
    as motifs, 52, 58
Designing for cross-stitch, 66-99
    by drawing, 66-91
    lines, 69-70
    with paper cutouts, 92-99
    patterns, 70-71, *72-91*
Designing for other stitches, 100-119
    enlarging patterns, 113-114

Faces and figures, 52
    patterns, *89*
    in samplers, 52
Flora
    as models, 7, 8, 10, 100
Flower cushion, spring, 11
Flower place mats, 19
Flowers and fruits
    and color, 90
Flowers of states of U.S., 39
French knots, *128, 129*

Gooseberry cushion, 29
Graph paper, 67, *132*, 133

Half cross-stitch, *124, 125*
    design for, 66
Hansen, Ejnar
    Guild dyer, 8, 29
Heath bedstraw cushion, 115
    pattern, *117*
Hem stitch, *126*
Herbarium specimens
    as models, 10

Ivy tablecloth
    design of, *75-77*
Ivy table mat, 51
Ivy wreath tablecloth, 18

"Lady and the Unicorn, The," 7, 9
    embroidery based on, *14-15*
Lady's-mantle cushion, 105
Linens, 120, *121*
Long stitch, *128, 129*
Long-armed cross-stitch, *128, 129*

Materials, 120-123
    linens, 120, *121*
    needles, 120, 121
    wool canvas, 42
Models, 10, 13, 100

Needles, 120, 121
Negative pattern, 11

Paper for design, 67, 133
Paper cutouts
    designing with, 92-99
Patterns
    drawing, 70-71, *72-91*
    enlarging, *113-114*

    negative, 11
    from paper cutouts, *92-99*
    for predesigned embroidery, 100, *101*
    repeating, 75-76, *77-81*
    supplier, 134
Perspective
    and color, 90
Plantain tea cozy, 105
Predesigned embroideries, 100
Pricking, 110
    enlarging a design for, 113-114
Primrose cushion, 22

Red currant cushion, 32

Samplers, old Danish, 52
Satin stitch, *127*
Schoolboys' cushion, 62
Schoolgirls' cushion, 63
Scilla doily
    design of, *83-87*
Song choir wall hanging, 64
    pattern, *65*
Spring flowers cushion, 11
Stem stitch, *124, 125, 127*
Stitchery, *124-131*
Stitches
    appliqué, *130*, 131
    backstitch, 66
    backstitched chain, *130*, 131
    coral, *127*
    cross-stitch, *124, 125, 128, 129*
    daisy, *130*, 131
    French knots, *128, 129*
    hem, *126*
    long, *128, 129*
    long-armed cross-stitch, *128, 129*
    satin, *127*
    stem, *124, 125, 127*

Threads, *see* Danish Flower Threads
    Clark, 120
    D.M.C., 120
Tracing paper, 67, 133

Virginia creeper cushion, 48
    pattern, *49*

Wild carrot cushion, 108, 112
    pattern, *113*
Wild plants wall hangings, 24-25
Working drawing, 68